Cell Phones

TECHNOLOGY 360

Cell Phones

ANDREW A. KLING

LUCENT BOOKS
A part of Gale, Cengage Learning

GALE
CENGAGE Learning™

Detroit • New York • San Francisco • New Haven, Conn • Waterville, Maine • London

LIBRARY OF CONGRESS CATALOGING-IN-PUBLICATION DATA

Kling, Andrew A., 1961-
    Cell phones / by Andrew A. Kling.
        p. cm. — (Technology 360)
    Includes bibliographical references and index.
    ISBN 978-1-4205-0164-3 (hardcover)
  1. Cellular telephones—Juvenile literature. I. Title.
    TK6570.M6K55 2009
    621.3845'6—dc22
    2009006249

Lucent Books
27500 Drake Rd
Farmington Hills MI 48331

ISBN-13: 978-1-4205-0164-3
ISBN-10: 1-4205-0164-X

Printed in the United States of America
2 3 4 5 6 7 12 11 10

Printed by Bang Printing, Brainerd, MN, 2ndPtg., 02/2010

CONTENTS

FOREWORD

"As we go forward, I hope we're going to continue to use technology to make really big differences in how people live and work."
—Sergey Brin, co-founder of Google

The past few decades have seen some amazing advances in technology. Many of these changes have had a direct and measureable impact on the way people live, work, and play. Communication tools, such as cell phones, satellites, and the Internet, allow people to keep in constant contact across longer distances and from the most remote places. In fields related to medicine, existing technologies—digital imaging devices, robotics and lasers, for example—are being used to redefine surgical procedures and diagnostic techniques. As technology has become more complex, however, so have the related ethical, legal, and safety issues.

Psychologist B.F. Skinner once noted that "the real problem is not whether machines think but whether men do." Recent advances in technology have, in many cases, drastically changed the way people view the world around them. They can have a conversation with someone across the globe at lightning speed, access a huge universe of information with the click of a key, or become an avatar in a virtual world of their own making. While advances like these have been viewed as a great boon in some quarters, they have also opened the door to questions about whether or not the speed of technological advancement has come at an unspoken price. A closer examination of the evolution and use of these devices provides a deeper understanding of the social, cultural, and ethical implications that they may hold for our future.

Technology 360 not only explores how evolving technologies work, but also examines the short- and long-term impact of their use on society as a whole. Each volume in Technology 360 focuses on a particular invention, device or family of similar devices, exploring how the device was developed; how it works; its impact on society; and possible future uses. Volumes also contain a timeline specific to each topic, a glossary of technical terms used in the text, and a subject index. Sidebars, photos and detailed illustrations, tables, charts, and graphs help further illuminate the text.

Titles in this series emphasize inventions and devices familiar to most readers, such as robotics, digital cameras, iPods, and video games. Not only will users get an easy-to-understand, "nuts and bolts" overview of these inventions, they will also learn just how much these devices have evolved. For example, in 1973 a Motorola cell phone weighed about 2 pounds (.907kg) and cost $4000.00—today, cell phones weigh only a few ounces and are inexpensive enough for every member of the family to have one. Lasers—long a staple of the industrial world—have become highly effective surgical tools, capable of reshaping the cornea of the eye and cleaning clogged arteries. Early video games were played on large machines in arcades; now, many families play games on sophisticated home systems that allow for multiple players and cross-location networking.

IMPORTANT DATES

1876
Alexander Graham Bell invents the first practical telephone.

1920s
First commercial radio station broadcasts. By the beginning of World War II (1939), broadcast stations are found around the world.

1890s
Development of the technology behind modern radio, by Nikola Tesla, Guillermo Marconi, and others.

1941-1945
U.S. armed services experiment with radio telephones during World War II. Following the war (1946), Bell Labs begins development of radio telephone networks for U.S. commercial use.

1947
"Technical memo" written by Donald H. Ring and other Bell Lab engineers proposes a telephone network comprised of cells.

1979
First commercial cellular network launched by NTT in Japan.

1850   **1900**   **1950**

1969
Pilot telephone system along Penn Central Railroad's "Metroliner" route shows that computer technology allows calls to be transferred from one cell to another without loss of signal.

1970
Bell Labs applies for a U.S. patent for a cellular telephone network.

1973
Dr. Martin Cooper of Motorola Corporation demonstrates first portable cellular telephone in New York City (April 3).

in the Development of Cell Phones

1981
First international cellular network, the Nordic Mobile Telephone service, launched in Scandinavia.

1983
Motorola debuts the "DynaTAC," the first commercially-available hand-held cell phone. Motorola and AT&T inaugurate their first cellular networks.

1984
Breakup of AT&T telephone monopoly in the U.S. (January 1). Dissolution leads to current U.S. telecommunications landscape of many competing wired and wireless phone providers.

2001
First commercial launch of "Third Generation" (or "3G") network in Japan, offering improved data transfer speeds through more effective use of allocated frequencies.

1980　　　　**2000**　　　　**2020**

1987
Nokia debuts its first portable cellular phone, the "Cityman".

2003
First implementation of 3G networks in Europe (March), Australia (April) and the U.S. (October).

2012
Expected completion of worldwide implementation of 4G cellular network.

1991
First all-digital ("second-generation" or "2G") network, based on GSM standard, debuts in Finland. By the end of 1993, over one billion subscribers in nearly 50 countries use GSM networks.

A Worldwide Technology

The cell phone is a marvel. The wireless technology behind it has revolutionized how billions of people around the world communicate. It was introduced in a few select areas in the early 1980s, and now the technology is used everywhere. People living in areas that were once considered too remote for wired telephone networks now have the ability to stay in touch wirelessly.

The cell phone's appeal lies in its seemingly ever-expanding capability. Today people use their cell phones for much more than just making phone calls. They can use them to store and listen to music, access the Internet, send and receive written messages, and take photos and videos.

The cell phone is an instrument of social change. It has changed how and when people communicate with friends, family, and colleagues. Some people only use their cell phones in emergencies or when traveling, but most people use them throughout the day as a networking and entertainment tool. The definition of "out of the office" has new meaning since cell phone users can now conduct business from anywhere.

The cell phone has changed how people access the World Wide Web and how they interact with other people. In the 1980s, the cellular telephone was a curiosity affordable only to a few; today, the cell phone is considered a necessity by many and affordable by almost everyone. In the past, using a cell phone in public brought stares from onlookers; today, it is commonplace.

The continued evolution of the cell phone is due in part to advances in miniaturization, to enhancements in computer capabilities and capacities, and to user feedback and demand. Consequently, the number of cell phone users continues to grow every year. By the end of 2008, there were an estimated 280 million cell phone users in the United States, approximately 85 percent of the nation's population. By comparison, in 2000, less than 35 percent of the U.S. population owned a cell phone.

In Europe, the number of mobile phones equals or exceeds each nation's population, as many people own more than one phone. In countries such as Israel, Italy, and Taiwan, the number of mobile phones equals 140 percent of the population. At the close of 2008, there were an estimated 4 billion cell phone subscribers, up from 3.3 billion at the end of 2007. Consumers bought 1.1 billion new phones in 2008 alone. And technology experts predict that number will only grow, as citizens in nations where traditional telephone service is unreliable, such as Bangladesh or Nigeria, opt for wireless services.

Although some people only use their cell phones in emergencies, most people use their cell phones daily to stay connected to family, friends, and coworkers.

The cell phone has indeed come a long way in a short time. If the past is any indicator, its future lies in increased interconnection. The phones of the future may interact with a wider variety of household devices, streamlining tasks or chores. They may offer new forms of entertainment or enable new forms of commerce. Each new advance will engender new questions and concerns, as experts from health, technology, and the law will debate how and where cell phones should be used and by whom. And, in the midst of all of these debates, each new advance makes them even more indispensable for billions of people around the world.

CHAPTER **1**

The History of the Cellular Telephone

Cell phones have a variety of names. Today's devices are most accurately called cellular telephones, but are commonly known as cell phones or mobile phones or, more simply, cells or mobiles. No matter what people call them, the devices are just the latest in a string of telecommunications innovations that stretch back to the 1800s. These devices would not be possible without several technological innovations that preceded them. Among these are the telegraph, the telephone, and radio.

Sending Messages: The Telegraph

Until the late 1800s, personal and business communications had been conducted primarily through two systems: postal mail and telegraph. Both were widely employed, but each had its restrictions. Postal mail was an efficient means of sending correspondence, but was hampered by the distances the mail had to travel. The expansion of railroad and steamship routes around the world decreased delivery times, but it still took several days for a letter just to cross the United States.

The telegraph system was a faster way to send messages. A message in Morse code could be sent immediately via

electric signal to any location connected by the copper telegraph wires. By the end of the nineteenth century, such cabling systems crossed continents and oceans. But to transmit such a message, it first had to be encoded by someone who knew Morse code. Second, someone had to be on duty at the receiving end to decode the Morse signals into everyday language and handwrite or type out the message. Lastly, the message had to be delivered by hand to the recipient.

The telegraph system's primary advantage over postal mail was its speed of delivery. Messages could be composed, encoded, and sent across an ocean or a continent, and the sender could receive a reply, while a posted letter was still waiting to be transported out of the area. But only the wealthiest businesses could afford to be connected to the system and to employ telegraphers to send and receive the messages. Around the world, thousands of telegraph stations employed delivery personnel—often preteen boys—to deliver the messages to wherever the recipients might be.

Sending messages by telegraph was faster than postal service, but it still required skilled telegraph operators to work the lines.

An Instant Response: The Telephone

The invention and development of the telephone in the last quarter of the 1800s was a communications breakthrough. Early researchers, such as Alexander Graham Bell, understood that sound travels through air and water as waves of energy, and they had developed ways to turn these waves into rising and falling electrical voltage. The telephone converted human speech into an electrical signal, and the signal was sent along a copper wire to a receiving station, where the rising and falling voltage was reinterpreted as recognizable speech.

Other innovators quickly realized the telephone's broader applications. It promised what neither the postal system nor the telegraph could: immediacy. Using the telephone, one individual could talk directly with another. There was no delay in the communication, as there was in sending a letter or a telegram and awaiting a reply. Using the telephone also avoided the risk of having a message wrongly decoded or misinterpreted.

Making Connections

Initially, telephones were used to link government facilities. Then, businesses that could afford the equipment paid to be connected to the network. Soon, the copper cables of the telephone network were being strung throughout cities and towns, adding to the maze of wires from the telegraph network.

Until the advent of electronics and computers, telephone companies employed thousands of operators in cities and towns who connected each call manually. The operators, who were often women of all ages, sat at switchboards with rows of circuit connections that represented each telephone in the area. They completed each call by connecting the electrical circuit between callers. For a local call, this was a relatively easy procedure. If you wanted to call your neighbor, you picked up your phone and the operator answered. You told the operator who you wanted to call, and the operator plugged a wire into the switchboard's connection for your neighbor.

Long-distance calls were more complex, and consequently more expensive, in part because of the time and labor involved. For example, if a caller in Boston, Massachusetts, wanted to call someone in Atlanta, Georgia, he or she first spoke to a local operator. That operator connected the call to a long-distance operator in Boston, who in turn spoke with a long-distance operator in Atlanta. The Atlanta long-distance operator then spoke with the local operator for the particular neighborhood where the call was headed. Finally, the local operator completed the circuit and connected the call to the recipient. Making the connection could take several minutes, depending on how many operators were involved and how busy they were.

Telephone calls offered the personal connection that postal mail and telegraphy could not. Access to a telephone meant not having to wait for postal mail or telegrams to be delivered. It also meant that communication was possible any time, day or night. And neither party of a telephone call needed to know how to read or write to keep in touch. Consequently, the telephone rapidly became the preferred method of communication. The use of the telegraph diminished gradually at first, and then precipitously as more and more locations were connected to the telephone network by the middle of the twentieth century. Postal mail, however, remained popular for long-distance communications due to its lower cost and efficiency.

At the same time that telephone companies were stringing wires and connecting cities and towns in nations around the world, electronics pioneers were experimenting with a way to communicate without relying on wires. The technology, which today is commonly called radio, eventually became a key piece to the development of mobile phone technology.

Wireless Transmission: The Advent of Radio

In the early twentieth century, radio pioneers, such as Nikola Tesla and Guglielmo Marconi, developed a wireless means of sending and receiving messages. Using the same principles of rising and falling voltage as the telephone, the early radio pioneers developed equipment that could generate and receive electrical signals from the air in particular patterns. Each pattern, called a frequency, had a unique number of sound waves per minute or second. Each rise and fall of a wave is called a cycle; as radio electronics developed, scientists developed signals that had thousands or millions of cycles per second. Originally called kilocycles or megacycles, these are now called kilohertz or megahertz, in honor of electromagnetic pioneer Heinrich Hertz.

Like the wired telegraph, wireless radio had both transmitters and receivers. Transmitters generated an electromagnetic signal at particular frequencies, to which the operator added an additional signal that carried the message. The other half of the technology, the receiver, was set to capture the first signal on the transmitter's frequency and then interpret the secondary signal to receive the message.

The early radios were at first an improvement on the wired telegraph. The first radio companies employed operators who encoded and sent messages much as telegraph personnel did, using Morse code. However, unlike the telegraph service, these companies closely guarded their transmitting frequencies. For example, a Marconi Company wireless set could receive and interpret signals only on a certain frequency; conversely, wireless operators from competing companies had their equipment set for other frequencies. And the two could not communicate with each other.

The new technology proved to be a particularly invaluable way to communicate with ships at sea. Emergency situations, such as the sinking of the ocean liner RMS *Titanic* in 1912 (in which over fifteen hundred of the more than twenty-two hundred people on board died), led to international agreements that enabled radio sets to receive and transmit signals from multiple frequencies. Rapid improvements in technology allowed voice transmission, and by the 1940s, networks of stations around the world broadcast music, news, sports, and entertainment programs to millions of eager listeners.

During the middle part of the twentieth century, radio networks and telephone systems reached around the world. Large numbers of homes in the industrialized countries had a telephone, and many had radio receivers as well. Far-flung communities in developing countries eagerly awaited the arrival of the telephone network. Even one phone in a central location, like a general store, would allow the citizens to speak directly with the outside world. The system, however, still relied on the same basic technology that had first connected communities at the turn of the twentieth century: a network of wires.

Radio and Telephone Merge

The years of World War II saw the rise of the first effective means of telephone operations without wires, called radiotelephones.

The radiotelephone used radio frequencies to establish wireless connections. These devices were used during World War II with great success. American troops used portable radiotelephone sets to communicate with headquarters and other units over FM frequencies. Tanks were equipped with the devices so that they could receive and send information while they were on the move.

The radiotelephones used by American troops during World War II were the first effective use of wireless telephones.

After the war, American Telephone & Telegraph (AT&T) decided to examine the concept of radiotelephones further. In the United States at that time, AT&T had almost a complete monopoly on telephone service and its related technology. Its research and development center was called Bell Labs, in honor of Alexander Graham Bell. Bell Labs personnel improved existing technology and tried to imagine the future of telecommunications.

In 1946 Bell Labs created a test market in St. Louis, Missouri, for the civilian use of radiotelephone technology. They wanted to develop a way for businesses, such as those involved in construction or deliveries, to contact their vehicles as they traveled around the St. Louis area. This system had very limited range and operated on only three FM frequencies. The radiotelephone devices were manufactured by Motorola Corporation, which furnished AT&T with most of its wired network equipment.

The wireless equipment was very heavy and required large amounts of power. The basic unit for a vehicle weighed 80 pounds (36kg) and consumed so much power that it could drain a truck battery in seconds if the engine was turned off. Nonetheless, the technology was a hit with businesses. They discovered the system enabled them to save time and money, as they could contact and send their vehicles from customer to customer without having each vehicle return to a depot or warehouse. The demand for access to the network led AT&T to build new networks in twenty-five other cities.

The technology required installation of transmitter towers on the highest points of land available to provide large coverage areas, and these transmitters used high amounts of electrical power to reach as many of the radio telephones as possible. However, the signals could not reach everywhere, and the limited frequencies meant that users could hear every other conversation on the network and often had to wait several minutes or more for a break in the chatter before they could start their own communications. This problem prompted Bell Labs engineers to propose a radical shift in the development of radiotelephony.

Birth of the Cellular Concept

In 1947 engineer Donald H. Ring and a team of other Bell Labs engineers created a concept that is recognized today as one of the cornerstones of cellular technology. Ring and his fellow scientists considered the future of wireless telephoning based on the limitations of coverage and power requirements. Examining the system's drawbacks, the team's concept was an alternative to high-powered towers on high points of land. The vision relied upon a network of dozens or hundreds of low-powered towers, each with a limited range and its own frequency. Each tower would provide a signal within its particular range. This area of service is called a cell (not to be confused with the word "cell" that is used to refer to a cellular phone).

According to technology writer Tom Farley, the concept had several advantages over the current scheme. He writes,

> To avoid interference, every cell site would use a different set of frequencies from neighboring cells. But a given set of frequencies could be reused in many cells within the coverage area, as long as they did not border each other. This approach reduced power consumption, made it easier to expand service into new areas by adding cells, and eliminated the problem of signals getting weak toward the edges of the coverage area.[1]

Despite its appeal, Ring and his team understood that such a system was just a concept for the future. They recognized that there were two inherent problems with creating such a network in 1947. The first was technological.

How Does a Cell Work?

The heart of engineer Donald H. Ring's concept was what we today call a cell, or area of mobile phone service. Ring and his team imagined a network of towers that created wireless coverage through a geometric arrangement of adjoining cells. After studying several shapes, they considered the hexagon as the most efficient. The towers in today's networks generate cells in this same shape, so that each edge of a tower's hexagon adjoins a hexagon from a neighboring tower.

A series of hexagonal cells provides excellent coverage with little or no overlap. It also allows for reuse of frequencies within a predictable pattern. For example, picture a simple map of a hexagonal cell site surrounded by adjoining hexagons at each edge. This ideal cluster of seven cell sites could provide coverage with just three frequencies. If the cells are numbered one to seven, starting from the top and proceeding clockwise with number seven in the middle, then cells one, three and five can use the same frequency because the cells do not adjoin each other.

Additionally cells two, four and six can use the same frequency.

However, the real world of cellular networks is much more complex. Thousands of cells usually exist in a particular area, requiring many more frequencies to accommodate traffic loads.

Thousands of Handoffs

While the cellular concept was appealing, the Bell Labs engineers had no way of implementing it. The theory called for a system that could pass calls from one cell's frequency to another, called a handoff. It also called for receivers that could interpret the switching without losing the signal.

At that time, both wired and wireless telephone systems relied on an operator sitting at a switchboard who made this exchange by hand. Ring's concept would have been impossible to implement with human operators, especially in densely populated urban areas with thousands of calls being made simultaneously.

The only way that efficient handoffs could be achieved was with computers. However, in 1947, a single computer was the size of entire room and was limited to tasks that today's handheld calculators perform with ease. The integrated circuit, which later evolved into the silicon chip which runs today's computers, would not be developed for another ten years.

The use of wireless telephones was delayed by the need to have human operators making handoffs manually. This changed with the use of computers which could make the handoffs much more efficiently.

Limited Bandwidth

The second inherent problem was the need for additional frequencies, or bandwidth. AT&T needed the new frequencies to improve the existing mobile radio service, as well as to develop the cellular telephone concept, as Ring's concept envisioned networks of hundreds of towers, each with its own frequency. This involved working with a branch of the U.S. government called the Federal Communications Commission (FCC). The commission was established in 1934 to oversee the use of radio frequencies in the United States. According to SRI International's Center for Science, Technology, and Economic Development, AT&T petitioned the FCC in 1947 for additional bandwidth, "but in a key event impacting the development of the cellular telephone, the FCC declined to act, preferring to reserve the requested spectrum for the burgeoning television industry."[2]

The FCC's decision reflected the ongoing research into the development of broadcast television, which exploded onto the American markets in the 1950s. Through the 1950s and 1960s, the FCC concerned itself with growing commercial and consumer demands related to television broadcasting. Meanwhile, a few Bell Labs engineers, and a small number of researchers at academic institutions, continued to work quietly on the cellular concept. Another request from AT&T for additional bandwidth in 1958 also was rejected by the FCC.

In the late 1960s mobile telephone service was still restricted to three areas of the broadcast spectrum: 35 to 43 megahertz (MHz), 152 to 158 MHz, and 454 to 459 MHz. By contrast, FM radio stations in the United States had been allotted the bandwidth from 88 to 108 MHz, and UHF television broadcasts (channels 14–83) were assigned to 470 to 890 MHz. The mobile frequencies were so overcrowded that the FCC decided to reexamine AT&T's request for additional bandwidth. A pilot program involving the Penn Central Railroad helped the FCC make its decision.

The Metroliner Pilot Program

In January 1969 AT&T, the U.S. Department of Transportation, and Penn Central created a pay telephone service on its Metroliner service from New York, New York, to Philadelphia, Pennsylvania. AT&T used towers along the rail line to create nine cells over six frequencies. As the train reached the edge of a cell, it tripped a switch on the track, sending a signal to a central computer in Philadelphia. A caller's transmission was then automatically switched to the next cell's frequency. This was the first example of the automated handoff system envisioned in Ring's concept. The Metroliner's riders found that the system allowed them to make phone calls to anywhere they chose; even newly inaugurated U.S. president Richard M. Nixon used the service and declared it a success.

The success prompted the FCC to approach AT&T with a proposal: If AT&T could create a workable cellular system for over-the-road vehicles (such as cars and trucks) within two years, the FCC would grant AT&T's request for additional bandwidth. John Winward, a radio engineer, recalls how Bell Labs personnel achieved the feat:

> There were seven of us on the field development team. We were up on the roofs in the cold and snow doing all of the grunt work to make the cell phone concept work. It was a lot of fun and fellowship, but no credit for our achievement. It was sort of like winking at a pretty girl in a dark room; we knew we were doing it, but no one else did.[3]

The network was a success. AT&T presented its findings to the FCC and then to Motorola Corporation, its partner in the venture. AT&T envisioned that the network would be developed in the same way the wired network had been: AT&T would handle the bookkeeping and Motorola would build the equipment. On December 21, 1970, Bell Labs filed a patent application for a cellular telephone network, more than twenty years after Donald H. Ring created the concept.

However, the FCC still took no action on the additional frequencies. In the meantime, Motorola started developing plans of its own. Motorola had already built receivers, transmitters, and signal processors and had thousands of taxicabs, delivery vehicles, and police and fire vehicles outfitted with their equipment. Motorola executives realized that a cellular network for vehicles using Motorola equipment, but run by AT&T, would generate subscriber revenue only for AT&T. So Motorola decided to use the data from AT&T and develop something new: a cellular telephone that could be used independently of bulky equipment in a vehicle, one that could be picked up and carried with ease.

U.S. president Richard M. Nixon used the Metroliner's pay telephone service and declared it a success. This service was the first example of an automated handoff system.

Motorola's Surprise

On April 3, 1973, a group of reporters in New York City met Motorola's Martin Cooper for a press conference. Cooper invited the reporters for a short walk along the nearby streets, and he carried with him a device that Motorola's engineers had built for his demonstration. It weighed close to 2 pounds (0.9kg) and contained custom-built, one-of-a-kind electronics. It was the world's first portable cellular phone, and Cooper demonstrated its effectiveness by placing his first call to Joel Engel, the head of Bell Labs.

Even though many individuals had worked to make that first call possible, today, decades after his demonstration, Cooper is considered the father of the personal handheld cellular phone because of that press event. Motorola's invention had surprised and amazed the technology community. The magazine *Popular Science* put the phone on its cover that July and theorized that New York City could be covered by a Motorola cellular system by 1976. All of this was contingent on FCC approval.

Cellular Catches Fire

From 1973 to the late 1980s, the concept of cellular telephoning became a reality. Companies around the world developed their own networks and devices. For example, the first fully functional commercial cellular network was created in Tokyo, Japan, with eighty-eight cells in 1979. The world's first international cellular network, the Nordic Mobile Telephone (NMT) service, launched in 1981, and it offered service across several Scandinavian countries. It was also the first to allow international roaming, in which mobile phones from different systems could access cells from any of the network's towers. In 1983 Motorola built a network centered on Washington, D.C., and Baltimore, Maryland; AT&T's initial network began in the Chicago, Illinois, area the same year. By 1987 the two networks were operating in the ninety largest markets in the United States.

At the same time, companies and government-run networks were developing their own systems. For example, in Germany, the first mobile network

Martin Cooper holds the DynaTAC, the world's first cellular phone which he debuted to the public in 1973.

was developed in 1985 by the fore-runner of cellular provider T-Mobile, the government-owned monopoly Deutsche Bundespost Telekom. The cellular company Vodafone began as a privately owned subsidiary of Racal Telecommunications, developing cellular service in Great Britain in 1984.

In the United States, nationwide development of a cellular network was slow in arriving. The FCC had allocated some additional frequencies for cellular networks in 1974, but then spent many years creating a wealth of rules and regulations concerning the technology. One benefit of this was that any American cellular phone would work anywhere in the United States. But a major drawback was that, by 1980, there were only fifty-four radiotelephone channels for the entire nation. There were 120,000 radiotelephone subscribers nationwide and demand was growing. According to technology writer Farley, "at least 25,000 people were on waiting lists for a mobile phone; some had been there for as long as 10 years."[4]

With the hope that mobile phones would eventually become a commercial reality, companies around the world began developing devices for the general public. Two of these early handheld devices received worldwide attention. In 1983 Motorola debuted the DynaTAC 8000X phone, which was based on Cooper's prototype. Its size, weight, and shape led to its nickname, "The Brick." But Motorola soon found it could not keep up with public demand, even though the device had the hefty price tag of $3,995. In Finland Nokia Corporation introduced the Mobira Cityman handheld in 1987; it received international attention when Soviet Union leader Mikhail Gorbachev was photographed using one in Helsinki, Finland, to call his communications minister in Moscow. Like the DynaTAC, the Cityman was a bulky 1.8 pounds (0.8kg) and expensive ($4,500).

But during the 1980s, the telephone landscape in the United States was radically altered. In an agreement with the U.S. Justice Department, AT&T agreed to give up its monopoly on local and long-distance phone systems. AT&T was divided into a variety

What Happened to All the Pay Phones?

Pay telephones were common in the United States and other countries throughout the first eighty years of the twentieth century. They could be found just about anywhere. Characters on TV and in the movies used them frequently. Clark Kent changed into Superman in pay telephone booths, and secret agent Maxwell Smart entered his headquarters through one. Then pay telephones disappeared.

For the phone companies, it was simple economics. Increasing mobile phone usage meant fewer and fewer people needed to use pay telephones. As the cost of maintaining them outweighed the revenue they took in, the telephone companies began to remove them.

According to the FCC, there were more than two million pay phones in the United States in 1997. By 2007, the number had dropped to just over one million. In that same year, AT&T announced that it would phase out its remaining 60,000 pay phones by the end of 2008. In June 2009, an AT&T spokesperson confirmed that except for a few small contracts expiring in 2010, the company was no longer in the pay phone business.

of smaller, regional companies. This set the stage for the variety of cellular telephone companies that dot the U.S. landscape today and the intense competition for cellular customers. It also led to a wide variety of mobile phone innovations, many of which are tied to advances in computer technology.

Technological Improvements Expand the Field

The great strides in computer technology in the 1980s were due to the development of microprocessors, silicon chips, and integrated circuits. Computers using them became smaller and more powerful, and mobile phone engineers were quick to recognize their value in their own field. According to the Center for Science, Technology, and Economic Development,

> the advent of integrated circuits...permitted the construction of small, low power and lower cost equipment, particularly hand held portable units. They permitted a much lower cost structure for cellular systems.... They

also permitted small hand held units to be designed, manufactured, and sold at prices that eventually fell to the point where these units became the predominant type of mobile unit.[5]

An additional improvement in cell phone technology came with innovations in battery design. The nickel-cadmium batteries that were used in everyday devices in the 1980s, like flashlights and portable radios, did not provide enough power for extended mobile phone use. For example, after just a few minutes of conversation, the DynaTAC's batteries were drained and needed to be changed or recharged. But the newly invented lithium-ion battery, first introduced by the Sony Corporation in 1991, carried a greater charge for longer periods. This allowed cell phones to be left on for hours at a time and users to have longer conversations.

In addition to improvements in the devices, networks worked to improve their services. They began erecting more cellular towers. The towers enabled mobile phone users to travel across large sections of Europe, Japan, and North America without being out of cell range.

However, many inside the cellular industry continued to underestimate the technology's appeal to the average citizen. Gerard Goggin, professor of digital communication at the University of South Wales in Sydney, Australia, notes that many companies around the world made the same supposition about cellular's future. In his book, *Cell Phone Culture,* he writes,

> It took some time for the portable cell phone to become widely adopted by companies and network operators. Even until the mid-1980s, there was a strong assumption among engineers, marketers and managers...that cell phones would continue to be installed in and used in cars, and that portables were not viable.[6]

Nonetheless, cellular phones continued to sell, and subscribers kept signing up for service. There were fewer than 204,000 mobile phone subscribers in the United States in 1985; just three years later, the number of subscribers had exploded to 1.6 million. By 1990, subscribers numbered 3.5 million. In addition, subscriber numbers in Europe continued to grow as well. The burgeoning industry was reaching a technological and public relations impasse.

Area Code Explosion

As late as the 1980s some U.S. area codes encompassed entire states; others were assigned to entire cities.

However, that changed with the demand for phone numbers for mobile phones, as well as for fax lines and modem connections. As more and more nontraditional phone numbers were assigned, the available seven-digit combinations within an area code began to diminish rapidly. The FCC relieved the stress by creating dozens of new area codes during the 1990s and early 2000s. Today many states have multiple area codes, and even large cities, such as New York and Los Angeles, have multiple area codes as well.

Popularity Brings Technological Challenges

In the late 1980s and early 1990s, mobile phone users in Europe were faced with a twofold problem. First, the allocated frequencies were becoming overcrowded, leading to calls that could not be completed or that were cut off in progress, or "dropped." Secondly, travelers discovered that the phone they had bought at home did not work in other countries. For example, a British phone worked on 900 MHz, but the towers of the NMT system in Finland, Sweden, Norway, and Denmark worked on 450 MHz. This meant the British phone could not communicate with NMT towers to complete any calls.

American users had fewer problems as they traveled across the United States. According to technology writer Farley, the limited frequencies allocated by the FCC meant that "the United States suffered no variety of incompatible systems. Roaming from one city or state to another wasn't difficult like in Europe. Your mobile usually worked as long as there was coverage."[7] Japan's system had been built by their telephone monopoly, NTT, and so had no conflicting frequency issues. But European networks suffered the public relations backlash of frustrated customers, who found a patchwork of incompatible frequencies from nation to nation.

The networks formed a study group called the Groupe Spécial Mobile (GSM) that included representatives of twenty-six European mobile companies. (Today the acronym stands for global system for mobile communications.) The GSM hoped to alleviate the problems of frequency overcrowding and incompatibility that were plaguing European cell users. In 1989 they proposed a way to do so that addressed the current problems as well as paved the way for cellular's future.

CHAPTER 2

The Evolution of Mobile Phoning

As technologies evolve, scientists and marketers create designations to distinguish the old from the new. In the world of mobile phones, the earliest cellular systems and phones are called 1G, meaning "first generation." First-generation phones used the same principles as the 1940s radiotelephones. They sent and received analog signals in the same radio-wave form as the earliest transmissions. Throughout the 1980s 1G networks used the analog system successfully, until the allotted frequencies became overcrowded. Call volume exceeded the networks' capacities and calls failed to connect or were cut off prematurely.

European users also discovered that their phones often failed to work as they traveled outside their home country, due to the incompatible frequencies that were used by other networks. In the mid-1980s, the Groupe Spécial Mobile (GSM) was formed to examine the problems and discuss solutions. In 1989 the GSM proposed an innovative fix to the problems of frequency overcrowding and incompatibility. It believed that cellular communications needed to move from analog to digital.

The decision reached by the GSM led to a revolution in mobile phone technology. In many ways, the GSM was following in the footsteps of computer developers, who changed

Intercepting Cellular Calls

Because early mobile phone calls were like any other radio signal, individuals with the proper equipment and the right frequencies could listen in on 1G mobile phone calls. This situation came to light through two famous incidents involving Great Britain's royal family.

By 1989, the marriage of Prince Charles and Princess Diana was in turmoil. In December, amateur radio hobbyists intercepted and recorded a conversation between Charles and Camilla Parker Bowles, whom he had met many years earlier, before his marriage to Diana. The call, which was widely publicized in England, was made late at night between Charles and Camilla, and leaves no doubt that the two were having an affair behind the backs of their spouses.

Later that same month, a call between Diana and James Gilbey came to light; she was talking on a landline and he was speaking from his cell phone in his car. The contents of the call made it clear that Diana was having trouble with many of the members of the royal family, and that she and Gilbey also were likely having an affair.

Digital encoding of cellular networks in the following years made such interceptions a thing of the past.

the way information was stored and analyzed in the 1980s. The GSM technicians discovered that their field could also benefit from advances in computer chip design, capacity, and processor speed. Various compression techniques made possible by a digital system would allow each cellular transmission to occupy less frequency space.

Digital Encoding and Compression

The first digital networks, and the phones that were designed for them, are today called second generation, or 2G, to distinguish them from the earlier analog (1G) phones. While 2G phones were able to receive both digital and analog signals, earlier 1G phones were restricted to the analog networks.

The processor within digital phones treats the analog wave signal in the same way that a computer treats information: by reducing it to the binary code of ones and zeros. The analog signal is encoded by a device called a vocoder. The vocoder first analyzes, or "samples," the signal strength approximately every twenty milliseconds, and then converts the signal to a stream of binary code that keeps growing as long as the signal is received.

The vocoder is part of a computer chip set called a digital signal processor. This processor uses a technique called compression to further reduce the information inside a cellular call, such as the caller's voice, the background noise, and stretches of silence in the conversation. Compression allows between three and ten digital cell phone calls to occupy the airspace of just one analog call.

One compression method is digital speech interpolation. The chip set is programmed to recognize the difference between conversation and silence during a call, and only transmits a signal during voice bursts. This allows other cell phones' signals to use the bandwidth during pauses, thus using the frequency spectrum more efficiently than before.

Cellular communications involve a pair of radio frequencies: one for transmitting and one for receiving. These frequencies make up a channel. According to technology writer Tom Farley, "879.360 MHz might be a transmit frequency and 834.360 MHz might be the receive frequency"[8] within a channel of a typical cellular call. An additional compression technique, called multiplexing, allows multiple calls to be packed onto a single channel. The user's phone recognizes the digital signal of its particular call and disregards the others on the channel, which reduces the overcrowding and interference found in the analog networks. Therefore, digitization enables networks to carry more calls and make better use of bandwidth than before.

According to digital communication professor Gerard Goggin, there were other advantages to digitization. In his book, *Cell Phone Culture*, he writes,

> Sharing of the radio spectrum could also be more efficiently managed through precise allocation of channels and transmission of data. The process of digital encoding and encrypting of the signal made it a more secure form of communication than its first generation predecessors, far more difficult to be intercepted (certainly by amateurs).[9]

"Not Even the Internet"

In 1991 the GSM introduced its digital network. Today, it is recognized by many in the industry as the standard–bearer for network development around the world. It has more

A smart phone that uses GSM, the standard for network development around the world.

than 2.5 billion subscribers worldwide. In the words of technology consultant Nick Foggin, "no other technology has had such a rapid and universal impact—not even the Internet. Today there are more GSM mobile phones on this planet than there are computers, and mobile phone users outnumber active Internet users two to one."[10]

The digital revolution had consequences beyond the European networks for which the GSM standard was developed. Other innovators around the world created digital standards since the GSM was introduced in 1991. For example, one technique, called code division multiple access (CDMA), is widely used by networks in the United States and around the world. In the United States, the switch to digital encoding meant networks were able to handle cellular traffic more efficiently than before, even as demand grew throughout the 1990s. Recognizing this, the Federal Communications Commission (FCC) granted requests for new allocations of the broadcast spectrum for mobile use.

In the United States today, subscribers have a variety of cellular providers from which to choose. All provide digital signals that are relatively indistinguishable from one another in terms of quality.

Expanding the Reach

By the beginning of the twenty-first century, the cellular phone had become more than just a remarkable new piece of technology. For many, it was their link to the rest of the world. Their phone helped them maintain appointments, manage businesses, and keep in touch with their friends, family, and acquaintances. These consumers wanted to be able to make and receive calls wherever they went.

Most urban areas around the world provide some sort of coverage, a territory in which a cell phone can communicate with a cell tower in the vicinity and transmit and receive calls. With the advent of digitization, cellular networks not only upgraded existing cell towers, but also began building new ones, as more consumers purchased new 2G phones and demanded increased coverage.

Mobile phone companies touted their coverage areas and competed to provide service in less-populated locations. Today, cellular towers can be found in such remote areas of the United States as Yellowstone, Yosemite, Grand Teton, and Grand Canyon national parks. In many urban areas, the original cells that were created during the 1G era have been subdivided into smaller cells with the addition of more towers to handle the increased load of calls.

In developing countries, such as Rwanda and Indonesia, cellular phones are becoming a more viable alternative to traditional wired telephone networks. According to journalist Richard Wray in the article "Half World's Population 'Will Have Mobile Phone by End of Year,'" on guardian.co.uk,

the reduction in cost of mobile phone handsets and the fact that in many developing countries the fixed line infrastructure is patchy at best has made mobile communications extremely attractive to consumers in developing countries and markets. The so-called BRIC countries of Brazil, Russia, India and China [which are home to fast-growing economies] are expected to account for over 1.3 billion mobile subscribers [by 2009].[11]

Towers That Do Not Look Like Towers

The construction of a new cell tower, however, is not always met with approval by those who live or work near the proposed site. Many object to the idea of a tall steel structure in their midst. Some think the towers are eyesores. Others consider them to be unwelcome lightning rods, while others are concerned

A cell phone tower disguised to look like a tree. Cellular providers have become creative in hiding towers in residential neighborhoods.

that they will attract their children's curiosity, putting the children in danger of electrocution. Consequently, cellular networks have become creative with new construction proposals.

One way cellular providers have become creative with tower construction can be found along U.S. interstate highway 85 near Greenville, South Carolina. The cell phone tower that rises above the landscape appears typical, with its steel-lattice structure and antennae near the top. However, this tower carries three sets of antennae, one each for three different networks. The providers decided it made more sense to build one tower with three antenna arrays than three separate towers in the same vicinity.

In September 2008 a cellular provider approached the Crystal Lake, Illinois, parks board with a proposal to lease a parcel of a neighborhood park for $2,000 a month. The company proposed to build a 75-foot (23m) cell phone tower that looks like a flagpole. In fact, the tower's design would allow the community to fly the park district's flag from it. According to the *Northwest Herald* newspaper, Crystal Lake Park District director Kirk Reimer felt the tower might be a good way to raise income and the design was the key. "Really the only thing people are going to see is a pole sticking straight in the air,"[12] he said. A number of nearby residents objected to the plan, even with the tower disguised as a flagpole. One said, "There's a place for the towers, and I don't think it's in the middle of a public park. Why are we subsidizing a commercial organization with our park space?"[13]

A similar pole, 80 feet (24m) tall, stands in front of John Burroughs Elementary School in Washington, D.C. It looks so much like a flagpole that local residents did not realize it was a cell phone tower until many months after it was installed. They protested, however, once they discovered the pole's actual purpose.

Cell Phones, Radiation, and Cancer

Both average users and medical professionals question if mobile phones are hazardous to human health. Specifically, they wonder if repeated exposure to the phones' electromagnetic radio waves may cause brain tumors and other types of cancer.

Currently, no research has shown a connection between mobile phone use and cancer. But most of the studies have only looked at short-term use—no more than three years. Israeli neuroscientist Sigal Sadetzki believes that long-term studies of children who are now growing up with cell phones may be the most revealing. In the article, "Do Cell Phones Cause Cancer?" published August 8, 2008, in the magazine *The Week*, Sadetzki says, "It takes at least 10, 20, or 30 years to see exposure to cancer." She says that it's reasonable to assume that whatever affects the phones have will accumulate over the years.

However, Sadetzki is not advocating banning cell phone use. She also says in *The Week*, "Nobody will stop using this technology. There are car accidents and still we keep driving cars. The question is, what precautions do we take?"

Citizens in other communities around the world have begun to question where cell towers are placed. Some, such as the citizens near John Burroughs Elementary, are concerned about the electromagnetic signals involved, believing there may be links between the signals and cancer. Others believe that the towers are a hazard to wildlife, particularly to birds that fly into them. And other citizens just feel that traditional towers are ugly. Following such citizen feedback concerning towers at or around schools, the Los Angeles Unified School District in California banned tower installations on school properties in 2000.

A Variety of New Tools

Despite concerns about where to build them, the growing number of towers has expanded coverage, making mobile phones more popular than ever. Consumers shopping for the new 2G phones also discovered that the devices offered more than just expanded coverage. In 1996 cellular company Nokia introduced a model called the Communicator. This GSM phone, initially marketed in Europe, included a variety of new tools, including a small typewriter-style keyboard and a

The Communicator by Nokia was the first cell phone to contain a variety of tools that would become standard on later generations of cell phones.

built-in word processing program and had the ability to send and receive faxes and e-mail. While the Communicator did not sell well in the United States, it served as a harbinger of things to come, as data capability became an integral part of mobile phones in the early twenty-first century.

For many consumers, the most valuable feature of early 2G phones was the address book, or contact list, that enabled users to record and store names and phone numbers. Other options allowed users to track who had called them and when; how many calls they had received, missed, and placed; and how long each call lasted. In addition, 2G phones also offered voice mail.

Each of these features enabled users to personalize their phones to their liking. The days of the home phone from AT&T, which looked and behaved like every other phone on the block, were clearly over. This became especially true with the rise of the ringtone.

From Beethoven to Beyoncé

As 2G phones became more sophisticated, manufacturers developed the first ringtones. These were simple digital files of melodies, such as Beethoven's "Für Elise" or Scott Joplin's "The Entertainer," that were easily recognizable in just single-note sequences. Although they sounded like someone using one finger to play notes on a piano, consumers enjoyed having an alternative to the standard ringing telephone sound, and it helped them distinguish their phone from other phones in a room full of people.

In 1997 a Finnish computer programmer named Vesa-Matti Paananen developed software that helped change the sound of mobile telephones around the world. His program, called Harmonium, allowed users to create melodies with rudimentary harmonic and rhythmic accompaniment on their phones. Paananen uploaded his development to the Internet, and soon people around the world were using it to create what is today known as the polyphonic ringtone.

In an article for *The New Yorker* magazine, musician and music critic Sasha Frere-Jones describes this innovation as "a small packet of code that plays the phone as if it were a music box, producing a synthesized approximation of a song that often sounds less like the original it emulates than a gremlin making merry inside a video game."[14] However, these were a significant improvement over the first ringtones, and their availability online made them even more accessible.

Users generally paid a small fee to download snippets of their favorite melodies and tried to determine which ringtone best suited their personality. An architect in her mid-thirties said,

> I spent three days of productive work time listening to polyphonic ringtone versions of speed metal, trying to find exactly the ringtone that expressed my personality with enough irony and enough coolness that I could live with it going off ten times a day. In a quiet room, in a meeting, this phone's gonna go off—what are they going to hear?[15]

The multitude of available ringtones enables consumers to change the melodies as often as they wish. For some, changing their ringtone may be just a matter of changing tastes or moods. For others, it is the desire to be unique—to be different from everyone else. In 2004 researchers conducted a study among Australians about how they viewed their phones. When one woman was asked about whether she saw this customization as an extension of the user's personality or identity, she replied,

> I think so because I think you get judged by your ringtone when you are in public. When you hear someone's ringtone that is the same as yours you expect to find your [double].... It (customizing) does become a fashion thing you get judged on.[16]

Today's ringtone consumers have greater choices than they did in 2004. The Internet has numerous ringtone sites from which users can download compressed excerpts of entire songs, called master tones, or true tones. Other users can create their own music snippets using audio software to create MP3 files which may be used as ringtones as well.

Another appeal of ringtones is the ability to choose when to hear it. For example, a mobile phone owner may download a song by Beyoncé as a ringtone for incoming calls from

How a Ringtone Works

The key to every modern cell phone is its microprocessor. This component controls everything the phone does, including how it rings to indicate an incoming call. A ringtone is a piece of computer code that sits on the phone's memory chip and is linked to the microprocessor's tasks associated with an incoming call.

When a call arrives, the microprocessor enacts a series of functions, such as turning on the display and showing the caller's number. These tasks are stored in the phone's memory; when a user installs a custom ringtone, its code gets added to the list of functions. The code tells the microprocessor to activate the phone's speaker system and to activate the piece of code associated with the ringtone.

The earliest ringtones were relatively simple bits of code, activating the speaker one note at a time. Today's polyphonic and true-tone ringtones are more complex, but they are activated in the same way.

everyone or for just one friend who is a Beyoncé fan. One American teen said, "Who doesn't like to hear their favorite song when a friend calls?"[17] Many users have programmed individual ringtones for the people who call the most—friends, family, and business contacts—so that they know instantly who is calling without having to reach for the phone.

The Business Side of Ringtones

Ringtones have become a huge business. The industry hit a peak in the United States in 2006, as sales hit $600 million before declining to $550 million in 2007. European sales reached more $1 billion in 2007, with industry experts estimating that ringtone sales accounted for nearly 30 percent of mobile phone content sales (which includes games, wallpapers, and other downloadable features).

Industry experts also believe there is a growing market for ringbacks, which is the next generation of ringtones. Ringbacks play as you wait for a call to connect, instead of standard ringing tones. And according to journalist Victoria Shannon writing in the *New York Times* newspaper,

> Jonathan Medved, chief executive of Vringo, said he believed his company had the next big thing in

the ringtone wave: video ring tones. Vringo, based in Israel, offers sports clips, cartoons, music videos and other shorts so that your call shows the animation of your choice when it rings on your buddy's phone.[18]

The ability to personalize one's phone has contributed greatly to the cell phone's appeal. Today, they seem to be everywhere. They have increased our ability to call and be called. And their pervasiveness has challenged societies around the world to define the boundaries of their use.

Questions of Etiquette and Privacy

In many countries around the world, it is common to walk through a store or a shopping mall and see people of all ages talking on cell phones. Friends call each other to arrange meetings. Spouses call each other with grocery needs. Business people call their office from airports, train stations, and taxicabs. In an article for the *New Atlantis* magazine, Christine Rosen of the Ethics and Public Policy Center in Washington, D.C. writes,

> What you never used to expect, but must now endure, is the auditory abrasion of a stranger arguing about how much he does, indeed, owe to his landlord. I've heard business deals, lovers' quarrels, and the most unsavory gossip. I've listened to strangers discuss in excruciating detail their own and others' embarrassing medical conditions; I've heard the details of recent real estate purchases, job triumphs, and awful dates.[19]

All of these situations not only challenge the perceptions of good manners and etiquette, but the perceptions of what is private and privileged information as well. Additionally, all of these perceptions change from country to country. In some cultures, there are definite places where cell phone conversations are considered to be in bad taste. For example, one researcher notes that various European cultures view mobile use differently,

BITS & BYTES

30 percent
Percentage of mobile phone content sales in Europe in 2007 that came from ringtones

reporting that "the French and Germans... are much more likely to regard leaving the mobile phone on in a restaurant as a faux pas, compared to the Italians, Spanish or English."[20]

The sheer numbers of cell phone users have led many societies to reexamine when and where mobile phone use is appropriate. For example, in many places where people gather, such as libraries and movie theaters, patrons are asked to turn off their phones. In many airports around the world, private booths are designated calling areas, much in the way that pay telephones booths once were.

Cell phone use is not limited to outside or private areas, but people can be seen using them in any public place. This brings up the questions of when and where mobile phone use is appropriate.

However, some individuals continue to use cell phones in these surroundings, despite a variety of signs, announcements, and other reminders about appropriate behavior. Professor James E. Katz is chair of the Department of Communication at Rutgers University, where he also directs the Center for Mobile Communication Studies. In his book *Magic in the Air,* he writes, "Ringtone complaints as well as their having grown so loud have caused some Mexican churches to have installed mobile phone jamming devices, preventing signals from getting through."[21]

For many individuals who are unwilling to be exposed to the conversation of others, it is often easy enough to relocate to another part of the building, store, or theater. However, a place with very limited space, such as an airplane, provides fewer options.

Flying with a Mobile Phone

Currently, cell phone use is prohibited on airplanes in the United States. The FCC originally implemented the ban to prevent possible interference between airborne passengers and wireless systems on the ground. Scientific evidence in the late 1990s also found that such devices could skew airplane navigation displays by as much as five degrees.

However, one regulatory agency's March 2008 decision means that cell phone users might be able to use their mobiles on European airlines in the near future. The British regulatory agency Ofcom, which is similar to the FCC, gave approval to such use once airplanes reach an altitude of 10,000 feet (3,048m). Shortly thereafter, the European Union's telecommunications commission and aviation safety agencies agreed to the proposal.

The approvals followed developments in technology that reduce the effects mobile devices may have on airplane electronics. The proposed systems would use a small base station, called a picocell, placed in the rear of the aircraft's passenger cabin. Each cell call would be transmitted to the base station. The base station would transmit the calls to a satellite for relay to the ground-based network. The picocell would use frequencies that do not interfere with the aircraft's navigational and communications electronics, and because the mobile phones in the plane would be very close to the base station, both the phones and the picocell could operate on very low power levels.

Radio spectrum across Europe has already been allocated for the service. Additionally, according to an article on the BBC News Web site, "flight captains would be able to switch off the on-board service if they felt it necessary."

For many cell phone users, having their phones work while they are traveling by plane would be a welcome benefit.

Calling a Person, Not a Place

The unexpected and unprecedented growth of cell phones around the world has led to its enthusiastic adoption by billions of individuals around the world. It is not uncommon to find homes in both developed and developing nations where three generations of a family have and use cell phones.

For many, the mobile phone has become the means of scheduling one's entire life. Swiss sociologist Hans Geser notes that among many users he has studied, patterns of long-term planning and coordination are replaced,

Mobile phones have allowed people around the world to streamline their lives.

What Do You Call Your Cellular Phone?

Around the world, portable communications devices using a cellular network take on different names based on the culture of the user. In the former British colonies of Singapore, Malaysia, India, and Australia, people talk about "mobile phones," with the emphasis being on their mobility. However, according to researcher Genevieve Bell in the book *Thumb Culture: The Meaning of Mobile Phones for Society,*

in Singapore and Malaysia, people also talk about *hand phones*; in China, *Shouji* [hand machine]—how the phone is carried is the relevant modifier in these contexts. In Indonesia, the label hand phone has been shortened to the initials *HP* and then re-interpreted through a more *Bahasa* [Indonesian] sound to *ha-pe.* More recently, in Australia, people have started to refer to their mobile phones as *my phone*, distinguishing from *my home phone*, where the home is now the differentiating modifier.

giving way to spontaneous, ad-hoc coordination according to current whims and circumstances. Social life therefore becomes more unpredictable and more complex forms of social cooperation may be more difficult to create and maintain.... [Cell phone usage] diminishes their capacity for keeping a separate private life or maintaining any other commitments.[23]

Many professional and casual observers of mobile phone use would disagree with Geser's assessment. Across the world, both sociologists and casual observers have discovered how mobile phone users have adapted the technology to streamline their lives. Sociologist Richard Ling is a senior researcher with the Telenor Research Institute in Norway. He notes, "The assertion that mobile communication fosters cohesion seems to be borne out in several studies."[24] Citing evidence from studies of users from countries including Japan, South Korea, Norway, and France, he says, "We are starting to use mobile communication to tie our family or our peer group together in new ways. We use this communications medium to interlace interaction within the group into our everyday activities."[25]

Microphone

The microphone picks up the caller's voice and transmits the information to the signal processor for digitization before it is transmitted to the network towers.

Speaker

The speaker is the last link in the cellular call chain. The digital information of the call passes through the signal processor and is returned to analog wave form and is transmitted to the speaker, where it is amplified into decipherable sound.

LCD or plasma display

The display receives binary input from the phone's computer processor that is displayed on the phone's screen as numbers, letters, words, and images.

Battery

The battery enables the cell phone to work without being plugged in to an electrical outlet. All of the power required by the phone's electronics comes from the battery.

Keyboard

Each key on the keyboard creates a particular binary signal; this signal is sent to the phone's computer processor where it is then sent to the display as legible type.

Circuit board

The circuit board houses all the electronics of the phone, including the digital signal processor, the computer processor, memory cards, and the radio frequency amplifiers.

Antenna

The antenna enables the cell phone's signals to communicate with the closest cell phone tower. Outgoing call information from the phone's radio frequency amplifiers passes through the antenna to the tower; incoming information is received by the antenna and is passed to the amplifiers.

For millions around the world, these interactions are what make their mobile phones such an important part of their lives. For example, in the Rwandan capital of Kigali, a self-employed auto mechanic explains how his mobile phone has made his business more efficient: "Before, when I wanted a spare part, I was supposed to go pick it up. But now I just call from where I am, and they bring it to me. Before, I would waste a lot of time."[26] In Malaysia, an information technology professional with five children says her phone enables her to better deal with the demands of both her full-time job and her family life. According to sociologist Genevieve Bell, "she relies on her mobile phone to coordinate child-care with her mother who lives next door, Koran lessons, after-school activities and meals, as well as to take care of various professional obligations."[27]

Ling believes that these examples show that a mobile phone is a tool used to manage daily life and how individuals use it is up to each person. For him, the key to the mobile phone is its ability to facilitate interpersonal coordination. He sums up the benefits of cell phone usage as, "you call a person and not a place, and that makes all the difference."[28]

Beyond the Digital Revolution

For millions around the world who use a mobile phone every day, the technology has helped shape how they spend their lives. Most of them give little thought to how the technology works, unless they experience a dropped call or find themselves outside a coverage area. The digital revolution helped bring cellular telephones to far-flung nations; increased computing power and miniaturization enabled users to personalize their mobile phones in ways that they never could with wired telephones.

But it was the brainchild of a systems engineer from Finland that led to the development of one of the most popular features of a mobile phone and one that has helped revolutionize communications. From its unheralded inclusion in the first GSM-standard 2G phones, text messaging has become an integral part of the worldwide mobile phone boom and an indispensable way for people to stay in touch, without ever saying a word.

CHAPTER 3

Text Messaging Goes Global

The digitization of cellular technology gave rise to the phenomenal expansion of the mobile phone and led to features that allowed for increased personalization, such as the ringtone and the contact list. In addition, the extraordinary popularity of one feature, text messaging, caught the telecommunications companies by surprise. Because it arrived on the scene at roughly the same time as electronic mail (e-mail), this feature swept around the world with unexpected speed.

The Short Message

In the world of cellular networks, the feature that sends and receives messages that appear on a cell phone's screen as typed words is known as short message service, or SMS. Today it is most often referred to as text messaging or texting. The technology is the brainchild of Finnish engineer Matti Makkonen, who in the early 1980s suggested the need for a simple messaging system for mobile phones. Makkonen's work on the evolving GSM standard included the function now called SMS.

The first text message to a cell phone was sent on December 3, 1992. A young engineer in London, England, named Neil

```
Do not want NEtin dat
belongs 2 sum1 else.
dun want ne1's house,
wife or husb&, slaves,
bullocks, donkeys or
NEtin else.
```

One of the Ten Commandments displayed in SMS. Originally thought to be a service to be used only by businesspeople, SMS—or texting—has become extremely popular with everyday cell phone users.

Papworth typed the message "Merry Christmas" from his computer keyboard and sent it to the cell phone of Richard Jarvis. Jarvis, the director of the telecommunications company Vodaphone, was attending a Christmas party in the south of England. The first phone-to-phone text message was sent by a Nokia engineer named Riku Pihkonen a year later, but SMS remained virtually unknown for several more years.

In circumstances oddly reminiscent of the telecommunications industry's initial assessment of how cellular telephony would be used, the cellular networks believed that SMS would likely be used primarily for business purposes. Indeed, only engineers and telecommunications developers used it for several more years. But a 1995 agreement between Finland's two leading mobile phone operators, Radiolinja and Telecom Finland, allowed their subscribers to send messages across network lines. SMS was suddenly available to everyday cell phone users.

Around the World

By the end of 2008, there were more than 3 billion SMS users around the world. In Pakistan, where there are an estimated 85 million mobile phone users, approximately 68 million text messages were sent per day during the first three months of 2008.

SMS usage continues to expand across the world. In the United States, there are an estimated 69 million text users; they sent more than 75 billion text messages per month in 2008. That equates to a rise of 120 percent over 2007. One network, Verizon, reported their subscribers were sending nearly five times as many text messages in 2008 as they had in 2005.

In Great Britain, the numbers are even larger. Users there sent approximately 79 billion text messages in 2008, or 217 million a day. The busiest day was New Year's Eve (December 31, 2008), when 398 million messages were sent that day alone. The annual figures are up from 57 billion messages sent in 2007 and 42 billion in 2006.

Clearly, millions of users have adopted SMS as a popular and, perhaps, a preferred means of communication. They have discovered that texting offers an especially convenient way to stay in touch using their cell phones. It has a number of advantages over traditional mobile phone use. For example, a user can send or read an SMS on his or her cell almost anytime, anywhere. The recipient's phone does not need to be on or within cell range for the message to be sent; the mobile's network will store the message for delivery as soon as the recipient's phone is back in range or turned on again. Using SMS is quieter than using a mobile phone for a traditional conversation, so it is suitable for places where a regular conversation would be considered intrusive, such as a movie theater or a library. Further, SMS messages can be exchanged across other wireless networks worldwide. And the messages themselves serve all manner of purposes.

"SMS Is Better than Trying to Call"

Text messages are as varied as the users who send them. Business people use SMS to send data around the world or to update their schedules. Mobile telecommunications engineer and media consultant Tomi T. Ahonen writes,

> So if I am in a taxi cab, suddenly in a traffic jam, and need to inform my meeting colleagues that I'll be 15 minutes late—the SMS is perfect. [Its] speed and efficiency of delivery is perfect... the SMS goes through every time...which is why SMS is better than trying to call and then playing voice-mail ping-pong.[29]

A variety of businesses use it for commerce and keeping in touch with their customers. Victoria Shannon writes in the *International Herald Tribune* newspaper that texts are used to "alert travelers to transportation delays, warn groups of people of weather and other emergency situations, advertise products and services, lend money and let you know if your bank account is overdrawn."[30]

BITS & BYTES

217 million

Estimated number of text messages sent by users per day in Great Britain during 2008

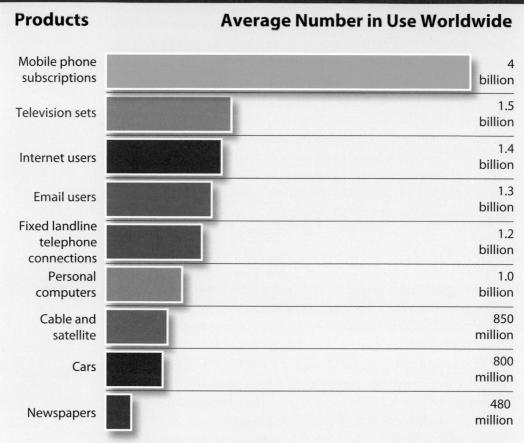

WORLDWIDE MOBILE SUBSCRIPTIONS COMPARED (2009)

Products	Average Number in Use Worldwide
Mobile phone subscriptions	4 billion
Television sets	1.5 billion
Internet users	1.4 billion
Email users	1.3 billion
Fixed landline telephone connections	1.2 billion
Personal computers	1.0 billion
Cable and satellite	850 million
Cars	800 million
Newspapers	480 million

Taken from: data from technology expert Tomi T. Ahonen, "Bigger than TV, bigger than the internet: Understand mobile of 4 billion users," February 06, 2009. Available at http://communities-dominate.blogs.com/brands/media/

The appeal of SMS may lie in its versatility. An ever-increasing variety of services are accessible via SMS. In the United States, pizza chains Papa John's, Domino's, and Pizza Hut invite ordering via texting. Texters in Indonesia can have their fortunes read via SMS. In South Africa, passport applicants can check on the status of their documents via SMS. Airlines such as Scandinavian Airlines, Germany's Lufthansa, and Malaysia's AirAsia allow flyers to check timetables and seat availability.

Farmers in Uganda and India can get SMS messages with crop prices to ensure the best time to bring their harvests to market. And researcher Genevieve Bell discovered that SMS can come in handy when you need it most. She writes,

> Everyone in Singapore jokes about the impossibility of hailing a taxi without a cell phone. Standing on Orchard Road one night in a sudden tropical downpour, I discovered just how true this was. Most public locations in Singapore now have some kind of code which you send in a SMS message to a taxi company who dispatches a taxi to your location—simple, but effective.[31]

But SMS is used for much more than just business. Around the world, it has become a common ritual of everyday life. Parents use it to stay in touch with their children across town, coordinating after-school activities and transportation. Men and women use it to arrange dates, to find romance, and to keep up with their spouses. And teens use it for everything.

Alerting Parents by Text

In 2005 the education ministry in the nation of Croatia worked with a national cellular network to create an SMS alerting system in more than one hundred schools. The system sends reports about the children's achievements and attendance to parents via text messaging. The reports also include information about the children's behavior, grades, absences, and completion of homework assignments. According to one school administrator in the book *Magic in the Air,* by James E. Katz, "if a child does not appear in school the parent will know within ten minutes."

Teenage Texters

Teens around the world have been using SMS since its introduction in the late 1990s. Many of those teens, now adults, continue to keep in touch with friends and family via texts. Mobile phone users in the United States came to texting later than others, due in part to mobile network restrictions. Consequently, the most prolific texters in the United States are cell phone users between the ages of thirteen and twenty-four, with a sharp drop-off for those between twenty-five and thirty-four. The older mobile users, on average, send less than half the number of texts per day as the average American teen. A survey by Nielsen Mobile of more than fifty thousand cell phone subscribers shows that the average American teen between thirteen and seventeen sent an average of 1,742 SMS messages per month during the spring of 2008. In one extreme case, a thirteen-year-old in California sent 14,528 SMS messages in the month of December 2008.

Teens use it to keep in touch with friends in the next classroom, to compare homework results in the evening, to gossip, and to say good night to sweethearts. One fifteen-year-old in Finland describes her texts as nothing particularly special: "Your basic, everyday messaging. Boring actually."[32] The impact of SMS is that these young people are able to stay in touch with their peers at all times, sharing their likes and dislikes, their challenges and triumphs, and their dreams.

But perhaps one of the most interesting aspects of SMS is how it has been incorporated into various worldwide cultures. It has helped reinforce cultural norms and helped bring people of similar interests closer together.

Overcoming Cultural Boundaries

Texting has been adopted by many users as a way of avoiding cultural missteps that may be found in countries with strict boundaries regarding relationships and status.

Many cultures around the world have well-defined boundaries concerning relationships and contact between individuals. What may be considered acceptable behavior in one culture can be a significant insult in another. SMS has been adopted by many users as a way of avoiding such cultural missteps. For example, in Japan, texting is used between people of different social status in order to avoid the social faux pas of interrupting.

Charles McGrath, writing in the *New York Times Magazine*, points out that texting allows users in China to take advantage of a mobile phone's basic design:

The Chinese language is particularly well-suited to the telephone keypad, because in Mandarin the names of the numbers are also close to the sounds of certain words; to say "I love you," for example, all you have to do is press 520.... In China, moreover, many people believe that to leave

voice mail is rude, and it's a loss of face to make a call to someone important and have it answered by an underling. Text messages preserve everyone's dignity by eliminating the human voice.[33]

SMS has also proven beneficial to groups of individuals who are living outside of their home communities. Some of these individuals are away temporarily, as their occupation takes them from home for short periods. Others have moved to a new region or a new country in search of a better life. Texting allows them to keep in touch with friends and family, without the concerns of time differences or the need for computer access for e-mail.

The Philippines is home to millions of cell phone users, many of whom are avid texters, and many of whom have friends and family who are employed in other countries around the world. Digital communication professor Gerard Goggin says that the nation is primarily an oral society in which speech is used to maintain and reinforce social status. For Filipinos, "texting combines the informality of speech with the reflectiveness of writing. Informants claim it is easier to express certain aspects of themselves by texting than through direct speech. They feel more in control."[34] This sense of control is vital for many mobile phone users. Being able to craft just the exact SMS gives them the feeling of being in control of their environment and their standing in their social circle.

Keeping the Faith

For many worshippers, a ringing cell phone is a rude interruption. However, in some cases, mobile phone technology is helping individuals follow their faith.

In India, some Hindu temples encourage worshippers to send SMS messages to the religion's supernatural deities represented by the shrine's telephone numbers. In Jerusalem, Jewish worshippers at the Western Wall (also known as the Wailing Wall) use their phones to connect to their friends and family at home. Holding their phones aloft while the other person prays ensures that the prayer is heard at that sacred location. Additionally, a cellular provider in Egypt launched a service for Islamic users that includes an alarm at prayer times and a directional finder to ensure the worshipper is facing toward Mecca.

A Tool for the Hearing Impaired

For members of the deaf and hearing-impaired community, texting provides another means of communication. At first, mobile phones were generally incompatible with telephone typewriter (TTY) technology. TTY technology uses a special keyboard and display unit that converts typed text into electronic signals that are sent via telephone line to another unit. In this way, the hearing-impaired could communicate with both hearing and deaf callers with the proper equipment. However, the advent of texting has changed how the hearing-impaired community views cellular phones. 2G cellular phones with texting capabilities have become, in the words of Goggin, "an answer to their prayers,"[35] as hearing-impaired mobile phone users "can take their means of communication with them as far as they can go and reach anyone who has a mobile phone."[36]

Scientists and educators have discovered that providing texting-capable phones to deaf and hearing-impaired students has enhanced the students' interactions with their peers, their parents, and their teachers. For example, a multiyear study in Toronto, Ontario, revealed a variety of benefits for students and parents. One student reported a rise in his self-esteem following learning how to text. The authors of the study say, "This is especially important as [this student] goes out of school on cooperative work projects. He has become an expert and is now helping to run further [texting] workshops for both students and parents.... He has been assigned as a mentor and role model for an elementary school deaf student."[37] A mother in the study group reported that her thirteen-year-old deaf daughter played soccer and hockey, was in a theater group, and was learning to sail and canoe. "You can imagine what is like trying to keep up with her.... [With texting] we have a system in place for checking in with each other... after school. I can let her know if I am running late, or need to go food shopping.... [She] in return can let me know how much homework she has and what her after school plans are."[38]

Protesters Organize Via SMS

The importance of text messaging in the deaf community was demonstrated in the fall of 2006. Students at Washington, D.C.'s Gallaudet University, the only university for the deaf and hearing impaired in the United States, used SMS as part of a protest campaign in opposition to the university's choice for a new president. The students rallied support for their cause from friends and relatives, many of whom are not hearing impaired, as well as from media outlets, using SMS. School officials were surprised at the students' organization and eventually acceded to their wishes, enlisting the students' participation during the search for a new president.

Social Circles

In many countries, the largest segment of SMS users are mobile phone users under age twenty-five. In developed nations, many of these users are attending schools and universities. The challenges of both school and growing up are the topic of millions of texts around the world.

Sociologists are studying how young adults are using SMS as a means of creating, testing, and maintaining social relationships in different societies. German researchers Joachim R. Höflich and Julian Gebhardt report that mobile phone users in Germany find text messaging useful in a variety of circumstances. One of the university students they interviewed prefers to send "a lot of text messages when I'd like to make plans to meet and always when it needs to be quick and I don't necessarily want a reply."[39] Another student felt that it was easier to flirt using SMS than by speaking to other people directly.

At the other end of the relationship spectrum is the break up. Young mobile phone users in France are using texting to end relationships. According to Richard Harper, principal researcher at Microsoft Research in Cambridge, England, a text message avoids "the possibility of emotional violence that goes with close relationships; thus girls would prefer to text their complaints to a boyfriend since this would not result in a physical outburst from the same boy; the boys prefer to text their own concerns since the girls do not respond with tears and weeping."[40]

Additionally, researchers examine how these individuals are able to cope with conflicting demands of class work, social relationships, and home life. For many, it is a juggling act they perform with ease.

"Just One Conversation? That Would Be Too Weird"

Molly Tokuda is a fairly typical American teenager. When she was interviewed by National Public Radio in December 2007, she was fourteen years

BITS & BYTES

15–20

Number of conversations maintained at once by average teens via SMS

Typical American teenagers are constantly texting with an ever-changing circle of friends about the who, what, and where of everyday life.

old and demonstrated for correspondent Chana Joffe-Walt how she used her cell phone. For Molly the key was keeping in constant communication. Joffe-Walt says Molly's rules for phone usage include telling her circle of contacts "where you are, what you're doing, who you talked to last, what you're wearing, what you'll wear tomorrow, and what just happened thirty seconds earlier."[41] Molly sat in the living room throughout the interview with her mother and grandmother, her eyes rarely leaving the screen of her phone as she texted almost constantly.

Naomi S. Baron, a professor of linguistics at American University, says that SMS studies show young people talking with fifteen or twenty others at once. She reports them as saying, "Just one conversation? That would be too weird." She believes this is because "you're supposed to keep all these balls in the air rather than be bored by 'listening' to one person's conversation."[42]

Baron says that many users like Molly are insecure about their friendships. "The fear is, 'If I don't get back, if I'm not sufficiently responsive to an invitation to go out to dinner or a movie, that person will move on to someone else, won't be my best friend.'"[43] When the Tokudas' next phone bill arrived, filled with fees and overtime minutes, Molly's mother disconnected Molly's service. She said that it may be that a mobile phone is a freedom Molly is too young to handle. Molly felt that, without her phone, she was cut off from her friends completely.

Molly, like many texters her age, discovered the allure of being able to keep in contact with an ever-changing circle of friends and contacts and had become adept at keeping in touch with them at all times. The automated features of 2G mobile phones allow users to reply to incoming messages immediately. And the rapid-fire nature of these conversations has given rise to a language unique to SMS.

"I Was VVV Brd in MON"

For those who do not use SMS, the language of text messages can be confusing at best and incomprehensible at worst. The combination of abbreviations for common phrases and apparently random symbols seem to be a completely different language. For example, consider this excerpt from an essay submitted by a thirteen-year-old girl at a prestigious secondary school in Scotland:

> My summr hols wr CWOT. B4, we usd 2 go 2 NY my bro, his GF & thr 3 : @ kids FTF... Bt my Ps wr so {:/ BC o 9/11 tht they dcdd 2 stay in SCO & spnd 2 wks up N... I was vvv brd in MON. 2day, I cam bk 2 skool. I feel v 0 : -) BC I hv dn all my hm wrk. Now its BAU.

In conventional English, the writer is saying,

> My summer holidays were a complete waste of time. Before, we used to go to New York to see my brother, his girlfriend, and their three screaming kids face to face... But my parents were so scared because of the terrorist attacks on 9-11 that they decided to stay in Scotland and spend two weeks up north... I was very, very, very bored in the middle of nowhere. Today, I came back to school. I feel very saintly because I have done all my homework. Now it's business as usual.[44]

For some observers, there is a distinct difference between the language of texting and the language of real life. Critics point toward abbreviations such as "yr" for "your" and "wat" for "what" in students' assignments as examples of the decline of standard English. Michael Bugeja, director of Iowa State University's Greenlee School of Journalism and Communication, believes that the texting shorthand

Vibrate Mode

One of the advantages of a mobile phone over a traditional phone is the ability to change how the cell phone rings. One of the features on almost every cell phone is a vibrate option. Users can turn off the ringing function and have the phone vibrate instead whenever a call arrives. Mobile phone owners have discovered that the vibrate mode allows them to keep their phones on in places where a ringing phone would be socially inappropriate.

When the vibrate mode is selected, the phone's microprocessor activates a small motor inside the phone when a call arrives. The motor drives a gear that has a weight attached to it off center. Because the weight is off center, the gear vibrates when it spins. This creates the vibrations that tell the user that a call has arrived.

QWERTY Keypads

In the early days of SMS, text messages were limited to 160 characters, and texters were challenged to create messages using the phone's numeric keys. Each key was linked to three or more letters and symbols; users tapped the keys to scroll through the options available.

Some texters today still use numeric keypads for their messages. Others have upgraded to expanded keypads that only contain two letter options, and others opt for keypads with each key assigned to an individual letter. These are called QWERTY keypads, for the first six letters in the top row. Additional options include phones that have keypads on displays or that can connect to external keyboards.

Users, of course, need to consider how they will use their mobile phone the most. Consumers who text a lot will likely look for models with QWERTY keypads. Others, who text rarely or not at all, will likely be happy without one.

encourages bad habits while contributing nothing to teen writing skills. When asked if any sort of texting helps writers with their skills, Bugeja says, "I don't even want to hear such nonsense."[45]

Others are not convinced. According to the April 2008 report, "Writing, Technology and Teens" issued by the Pew Internet & American Life Project, 75 percent of the teens in the study believe that most texts are not really examples of writing. Matt Carlson, an assistant professor of communications at St. Louis University, believes texting is merely communicating, and "there's a difference between writing and communicating."[46]

Steve Jones, a professor of communications at the University of Illinois at Chicago, is confident that if teens are able to distinguish between texting and writing, then they should not have any problems. He says, "I'm not too worried. It is absolutely critical to be able to write. But there are other mediums of communication they'll need to able to express themselves in."[47] And Goggin points out that "there are now a number of studies that suggest that text messaging does not have the direct and baleful effects on language competency and literacy suggested by detractors."[48]

Regardless of how SMS messages appear, there also are concerns about how and where the billions of text messages are composed. Increasingly, text messages are being sent from locations that may put the safety of the texter and others at risk.

Safety Concerns

The physical act of sending an SMS requires coordination of several different muscle groups. The user has to choose the proper keys to press on the mobile phone and watch the message forming on the screen. Texting also requires significant mental concentration. Ideally, the texter is in an environment without distractions.

But, increasingly, cell phone users are sending text messages from wherever they happen to be. Many environments demand the user's attention, and scientists are discovering that users often give more attention to texting than to their surroundings.

Across the United States, emergency room doctors are seeing a rise in injuries to people who send SMS messages while doing a variety of other tasks. Some texters, called textwalkers, walk and text at the same time. They suffer injuries stumbling on cracks in the pavement, falling off curbs, or walking into lampposts or walls. One young texter, a fifteen-year-old girl, suffered head and neck injuries after she fell off her horse while texting. A thirty-nine-year-old man suffered a head injury when he crashed his bicycle into a tree while texting. And a thirteen-year-old girl suffered burns on her stomach, arms, and legs after texting her boyfriend while cooking noodles.

Angela Gardner is an assistant professor in the Department of Emergency Medicine at the University of Texas Medical Branch in Galveston. She said she usually learns that her patient's injuries were caused by texting from the ambulance crew, not the injured patient. Her belief is "people don't want to admit they were doing something so silly."[49] Janet Armentor-Cota, an assistant professor of sociology at California State University Bakersfield, says injuries suffered while texting can be linked to the lure of the instant connection. "There's a culture being fostered here about always being in contact, always being accessible, [but in] the real world, there's the danger of falling off the horse."[50]

A large part of the allure of SMS is its speed and ease of use. Skilled texters can send and get responses to their messages in a matter of seconds. But this leads some users to attempt texting while doing other activities, such as driving, believing that they can do both safely. This practice puts the safety of both the driver and others at risk.

Texting while Driving

Drivers have a variety of variables to consider while operating a motor vehicle, including their speed, the condition of the road, and the behavior of other drivers. Many scientists and law enforcement personnel believe that using a cell phone while driving causes "distracted driving" and impairs the judgment of the driver.

A September 2008 survey by the American Automobile Association Foundation for Traffic Safety reports that 48 percent of people between the ages of eighteen and twenty-four acknowledged they have sent a text message while driving. A 2008 survey by Nationwide Insurance found nearly 40 percent of cell phone users between the ages of eighteen and thirty text and drive. And a Zogby poll found that 66 percent of eighteen- to twenty-four-year-old drivers admitted to sending texts while driving.

Some texting drivers have even broadcast their prowess at multitasking. A June 2008 article in *Time* magazine documents the practice, and includes an interview with a student named Taylor Leming, who created a social group on the online networking site Facebook called I Text Message People While Driving and I Haven't Crashed Yet! The group has more than doubled in size since publication of the article, and other groups debating the practice also have been created. Leming says she created the group mostly as a joke among friends following a discussion of their own texting-while-driving incidents. She says, "My friends and I were laughing about how we sometimes text and drive, and how we know

Texting while driving can have serious consequences such as injury or death to drivers or others on the road.

it's dangerous and have nearly rear-ended people because of it.... A few times, I was texting in stop-and-go traffic and had to slam my brakes to avoid rear-ending the person in front of me."[51]

Texting while operating vehicles can have even more serious consequences than injuries to the person texting. Across the United States, texting while driving has been cited as a likely factor in a number of fatal accidents. For example, in September 2006, a twenty-one-year-old Utah resident collided with a vehicle while texting. The two occupants of the other vehicle were killed. In January 2008, a thirteen-year-old in Massachusetts was riding his bicycle when he was struck and killed by a texting driver.

One of the most well-known incidents in which texting was involved occurred on September 12, 2008, when a Los Angeles Metrolink commuter train ran through a stop signal and plowed into an oncoming freight train, resulting in 138 injuries and 25 deaths. One of the fatalities was the Metrolink engineer, who apparently had been sending and receiving text messages up until the minute before the collision.

As more accidents occur, there are more calls from the public for action to prevent future incidents. Proponents of restricting cell phone use in cars equate their cause to successful efforts to toughen drunk-driving laws. Consequently, states across the United States have responded with new laws concerning mobile phone use in general and SMS use in particular.

A Growing Movement

Laws concerning mobile use vary from state to state and may change with each legislative session, as lawmakers respond to constituents' feedback and to new trends. For example, legislators in Illinois and other states are debating if textwalkers should be viewed in the same light as jaywalkers—as posing a hazard to themselves and others and therefore subject to a fine.

However, the use of mobile phones by drivers has received more attention than textwalking. As of 2009, five states (California, Connecticut, New York, New Jersey, and

STATE RESTRICTIONS ON CELL PHONE USE WHILE DRIVING

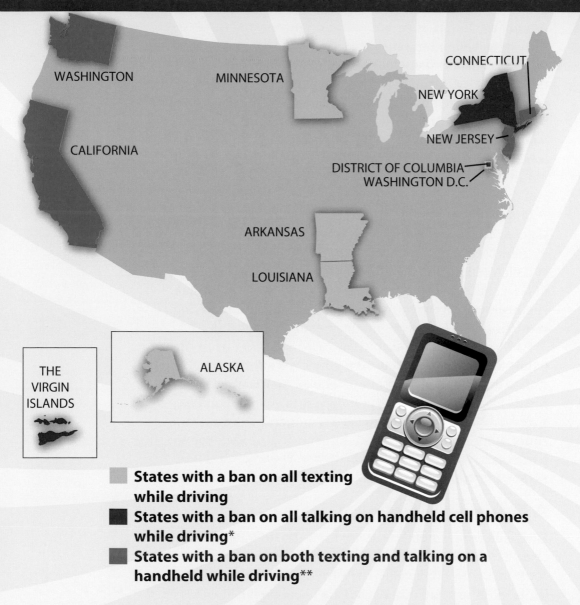

WASHINGTON

MINNESOTA

CONNECTICUT

NEW YORK

CALIFORNIA

NEW JERSEY

DISTRICT OF COLUMBIA
WASHINGTON D.C.

ARKANSAS

LOUISIANA

THE
VIRGIN
ISLANDS

ALASKA

States with a ban on all texting while driving

States with a ban on all talking on handheld cell phones while driving*

States with a ban on both texting and talking on a handheld while driving**

*Under these laws, police officers can ticket drivers solely for using a handheld mobile phone while driving. No other traffic violation needs to be cited.

**Under these laws (except for Washington), police officers can ticket drivers solely for using a handheld mobile phone or texting while driving. No other traffic violation needs to be cited.

Taken from: Data compiled by GHSA from the American Automobile Association (AAA), Insurance Institute for Highway Safety (IIHS) and State Highway Safety Offices. Most recently reviewed by GHSA in October, 2008. Available online at **http://www.ghsa.org/html/stateinfo/laws/cellphone_laws.html**

Washington), the District of Columbia, and the U.S. Virgin Islands prohibit all drivers from talking on handheld cell phones while driving. (Talking on a mobile phone with a hands-free device is permitted.) Seventeen states and the District of Columbia ban all cell phone use for novice drivers, usually defined as drivers under eighteen.

Text messaging laws are more widespread. Eight states (Alaska, Arkansas, California, Connecticut, Louisiana, Minnesota, New Jersey, and Washington) and the District of Columbia ban SMS use by all drivers. Nine others (Delaware, Maine, Maryland, Nebraska, North Carolina, Oregon, Texas, Virginia, and West Virginia) ban its use by drivers under eighteen, or who have a learner's permit. Texas bans texting for all drivers for the first six months of having a license, regardless of age.

Several other states are contemplating some sort of ban on cell phone use or SMS use within their jurisdictions or changes to existing laws. For example, Rhode Island's legislature passed a handheld mobile phone ban in 2001, but it was vetoed by the governor. Since then, a new law banned cell phone use for drivers under eighteen, and legislators continue to debate prohibiting SMS use and associated penalties. Discussions to ban texting or simply using a handheld mobile phone while driving occurred in several states in 2008, including Tennessee, North Dakota, and Illinois.

Taylor Leming, who created the Facebook group I Text Message People While Driving and I Haven't Crashed Yet!, believes she would support a ban on SMS use behind the wheel but feels enforcing it would be a challenge for law enforcement. "It would be a hard rule to enforce, as a cop cannot necessarily see someone texting while driving... [I] would feel pretty horrible if something happened because of me breaking a law."[52]

Penalties for Breaking the Law

Penalties for violating vehicle-related cell phone or SMS statutes vary across the United States. For example, in New York, using a handheld cell phone can result in a fine of up

When Reckless Driving Causes Death

Two recent cases reflect the differences in state laws regarding texting and reckless driving and how they are interpreted and applied. In November 2008, a plea agreement was reached in the case of Craig Bigos, a Massachusetts driver who was texting when he struck and killed a teen on his bicycle. Massachusetts does not ban the use of mobile phones while driving. However, Bigos pled guilty to motor vehicle homicide and leaving the scene of an accident in exchange for a sentence of 2.5 years in prison. In January 2009, the case of Reggie Shaw, a Utah man who was texting when he collided with a vehicle causing two deaths, resulted in a plea agreement as well. The investigation was delayed for a year as prosecutors attempted to retrieve Shaw's text messages from his phone provider. The message logs showed that he had been texting at the time of the impact. Shaw pled guilty to two counts of negligent homicide, which in Utah is punishable by up to a year in prison. As part of Shaw's sentence, he must participate in a public service antitexting-while-driving campaign and present his story to the Utah legislature. He is helping to spearhead new efforts to pass legislation that defines texting while driving as similar to driving under the influence of alcohol and subject to the same penalties.

to $100.00. First-offense fines in California start at $76.00 and rise to $175.00 for each subsequent offense. However, most statutes involve fines only; unlike driving-under-the-influence laws, violators receive no restrictions on their licenses or changes to their insurance policies.

However, the growing number of incidents in which cell phone or SMS use is involved causes concern among both legislators and lawyers. Attorney Stephanie Rahlfs believes that even in a state that does not have a ban on texting while driving, there could be other legal considerations following an accident in which texting was involved. "In the case of a traffic accident, proof that the driver was texting while driving may be used to help prove liability for the accident... it's conceivable that a jury could consider texting while driving as negligent or even reckless conduct."[53]

When a case involving cell phone use or SMS use behind the wheel comes before a court, judges and juries need to interpret the intent and application of existing statutes. A reckless conduct verdict may result in a fine equal to the cost to repair another vehicle or structure, a loss of driving privileges, or confiscation of one's vehicle. Reckless conduct penalties are more severe and may involve prison sentences, particularly if the accident results in severe injuries or death.

Clearly, as more drivers use mobile phones, they need to understand the risks involved and the consequences of their actions. As mobile phone technologies evolve, definitions of acceptable behavior evolve as well. Law enforcement authorities have scrutinized how and where cell phones are used, and many have decided to legislate appropriate times and places for their use. The challenge for them and for society at large remains to understand how the world of mobile phones is changing and expanding and how best to deal with it.

CHAPTER 4

Cameras, Video, and the Web

By the end of the twentieth century, mobile phones bore little resemblance to their predecessors from even ten years earlier. They were smaller and lighter, due to advances in miniaturization and increased chip set speeds. They also offered increased memory for saving contact lists and phone numbers. New features of the phones included greater display size, full-color screens, SMS capability, and a variety of ringtones.

However, cell phone developers continued to find ways to integrate other aspects of modern life into their devices. One of the most innovative functions now widely available inside a cell phone is a camera.

Camera Phones

By 1997 several companies were tinkering with the idea of integrating a camera with a cell phone, but it was technology developer Philippe Kahn who succeeded. The invention came as an inspiration during the birth of his first child. While his wife was in labor for eighteen hours, Kahn found a way to integrate his laptop, digital camera, and cell phone. He says, "I'd gone to the Lamaze classes... And the second time I said, 'Breathe!' Sonia said, 'Shut up!' So I said, 'OK, I'll sit at this desk and find something to do.'" So while his wife was in labor, he played around with the equipment he had with him. "I had time to make a couple trips to RadioShack to get soldering wire," Kahn says. "I just stayed in the room and made that thing work."[54]

Kahn realized how time-consuming it was to take a digital picture with his camera, send it to his computer, upload it to a Web site, and then e-mail everyone to tell them where it was. The process was relatively new at the time, but Kahn wanted to streamline it. And according to technology writer Kevin Maney, "by the time he was holding his newborn daughter, Kahn could use his jerry-rigged contraption to take a digital photo and wirelessly post it for his friends and family."[55]

A woman demonstrates the J-Phone, the first mobile phone to have a built-in camera.

At the time, Kahn was in the process of selling Starfish, his cell phone software company, to technology giant Motorola. However, Motorola was not interested in the idea of a camera inside a cell phone. So Kahn formed a new company called LightSurf to develop the software behind the technology. His work with Japanese manufacturers led to the first commercially available mobile phones with cameras.

In 2000 the Japanese company J-Phone introduced a mobile phone called the J-SH04, the first to have a built-in camera. Public reaction was mixed. Improvements in battery life and in picture resolution soon swayed Japanese consumers, and within three years, fully 90 percent of cell phones sold in Japan had cameras. The technology reached American and European consumers in 2002 and has helped transform how society looks at photography.

Micheal McLaughlin is a professional photographer in New York City. He believes that the accessibility of camera phone photography "has refined the medium." He feels that cell phone camera photography comprises another category of fine art, along with traditional photography, sculpture, and others; in his view, people can enjoy those images "as equally as a photograph made with an 8x10 [large format camera]." In addition, "traditional photojournalism is certainly being challenged, if not vanquished, by cell phone cameras."[56] News outlets now regularly solicit cell phone images from individuals who happen to witness news events; their point-and-shoot pictures enable them to become amateur photojournalists. And they can do it all with the mobile phone already in their pocket.

The Mundane and the Momentous

Most people do not carry a camera around with them all the time. They usually take one when they go on trips or attend special events, like a birthday party or a concert. But for those who carry their cell phone everywhere, the camera function of their phone allows them to take pictures without the need for separate equipment and without the need to plan ahead. The ability to send photos in an e-mail or directly upload the photos to a Web site makes taking pictures all the more fun.

Today, photo-sharing Web sites allow people to upload their pictures in a matter of seconds. These pictures may seem terribly mundane to outside observers—photos of friends enjoying a party, a newborn baby, a fish caught in a stream—but they have great significance for those who shot them. They are a way of recording everyday events that is more spontaneous than traditional photography, that is more instantaneous than a diary or a journal, and that is immediately available to almost anyone.

On the other hand, cameras in cell phones also have enabled users to document newsworthy events. On July 7, 2005, three explosions from terrorist bombs rocked London's Underground subway system. The explosions killed fifty-two commuters, including the four bombers, and injured more than seven hundred. Riders caught in the trains when the explosions hit used their phones to take pictures of the event. The British Broadcasting Corporation (BBC) received approximately one thousand images by e-mail from individuals who had been caught in the mayhem.

BITS & BYTES

90 percent

Percentage of cell phones sold with cameras in Japan in 2003

Less than six months later, an accident at a fuel depot, also in Great Britain, demonstrated the public's increased awareness of the value of such images. The December 2007 explosion was caused by an overfilled tank, and the BBC received more than six thousand photos; the first reached the BBC just minutes after the initial explosion. Pete Clifton, who was in charge of BBC News Interactive at the time, said, "The range of material we received from our readers was absolutely extraordinary,"[57] and that the photos "played a central part in the way we reported the unfolding events."[58]

Clandestine Photography

Not all camera phone images are taken with an eye toward journalism or assisting law enforcement. Unfortunately, cameras in cell phones have been used to take pictures in inappropriate places or of individuals without their permission. The challenge for society is defining the bounds and expectations of personal privacy, formulating policies for enforcing current laws, and enacting new legislation to meet changing technologies.

It has been difficult for authorities to restrict the use of cell phones with cameras in such public places as beaches. In some instances people have used these phones to take comprising photos of beach goers.

In some cases, businesses are able to police their establishments to suit their customers. Over the years, some people used their cameras to take pictures of other people in changing areas or shower facilities in schools and health clubs. This prompted many such establishments to prohibit all cell phones. Other cases, involving public places, present other challenges. Some people have used their phones to take pictures of people at clothing-optional beaches. In December 2004, an Australian man was convicted for having taken seventy-five pictures of topless women at a popular beach south of Sydney. As the man strolled along the beach, pretending to be talking on his mobile phone, he paused occasionally to use its camera. He was caught when one woman's boyfriend became suspicious and demanded to

An Unusual Mug Shot

In August 2008 a woman in New York City was carrying several items as she climbed the stairs to an elevated train station when she sensed someone standing too close to her on the stairs. The woman turned and saw a man looking into his mobile phone. As Christine Hauser writes in the *New York Times*, "a passer-by confirmed her suspicion: The man had taken photographs under her skirt. 'I said I had to do something,' the woman said.... 'Since he is taking pictures of me, I am going to take pictures of him.'"

The woman followed the man onto the train, and took a picture of him with her cell phone camera. He looked at her and mumbled something. "And I told him 'smile' because I am going to the police," she said.

The woman e-mailed the photo to the police and filed a report. Her photograph led police to a thirty-six-year-old suspect, who was arrested and arraigned on misdemeanor charges of unlawful surveillance, attempted sexual abuse, and harassment.

see the phone. The Australian man was fined approximately $400 and his phone was confiscated and destroyed.

The vast majority of cell phone camera users take pictures of purely fun or personally important events. And because most cell phone cameras also have motion picture capabilities, mobile phone users also can shoot videos for the same reasons.

Caught on Video

The first camera phone videos had poor resolution and contained far fewer frames per second than even budget video cameras of the day. It meant that what the photographer saw was rarely accurately translated into video; the images were grainy and objects in motion appeared to move in stops and starts. But by the time of the London Underground bombings in 2005, the technology had improved significantly. Victims trapped inside the trains not only took photos, but they also took video footage of the event and sent the footage to the BBC, as well as to photo-sharing Web sites. One grainy recording of survivors escaping through a smoke-filled train was uploaded to a blog and was later reshown by many media services around the world, without crediting the photographer. (Today, many who create cell phone videos use editing software to add copyright information, protecting their creations.)

Since the London Underground bombings, cell phone videos have captured a variety of landmark events, from the December 2006 execution of Iraqi dictator Saddam Hussein to the January 2009 inauguration of President Barack Obama.

Video Sharing

For mobile phone users wishing to share their videos with others, there are dozens of Web sites on the Internet where video creators can upload their footage. Some sites charge fees for the service, others promise a share of revenue generated by advertising traffic, and still others are completely free to use. These sites contain both amateur and professional quality videos, and many have been shot with cell phone cameras. A large number of these are videos shot at parties, sporting events, or behind the scenes at concerts. Perhaps the most popular of these sites is YouTube, which debuted in 2005. Like other trade names, such as Xerox or Kleenex, YouTube has become synonymous with video sharing.

One example of a cell phone video that was created for a Web site is one shot for soul musician John Legend's Web site. Using a Nokia N95 camera phone and a Web-based streaming service, one of Legend's staff created an eleven-minute video of Legend on January 18, 2009, as he stood on the steps of the Lincoln Memorial in Washington, D.C. along with such celebrities as Queen Latifah, Tom Hanks, Denzel Washington, Josh Groban, and Mary J. Blige. The memorial was the site of a concert celebrating the upcoming inauguration of President Barack Obama. In the video, the president-elect and his wife Michelle, along with Vice-President-Elect Joe Biden and his wife, talk to the artists, thanking them for the concert. The video is a fascinating look at the event; Chris Gaither wrote in the *Los Angeles Times* newspaper, "this unorthodox instance of citizen journalism (not every citizen hobnobs with political and cultural royalty) offers a creaky window into the top tiers of the nation's biggest celebration."[59]

Becoming a Cell Phone Applications Developer

Job Description: Cell phone applications developers specialize in the development of new software for mobile phones. The applications developer is responsible for designing, building, testing, and implementing the new application software, as well as the technical specifications associated with each new application.

Education: A bachelor of science degree in computer science, math, or electrical engineering is often required. Some employers will accept equivalent on-the-job training in lieu of a college degree.

Qualifications: Applications developers must have a working knowledge of a variety of computer platforms, including Windows and Linux/Unix, and programming and development languages, including Java, C/C++, and Brew.

Experience in wireless technologies such as Bluetooth is a plus. Additional experience in applications or game development, including graphic user interfaces, will be required for certain positions. Specific development experience for the small space of mobile phones is particularly valuable.

Additional Information: Some employers require experience on particular models of mobile devices, such as BlackBerry, iPhone, or Android. Applications developers are expected to be innovative and creative, to be able to work both individually and as part of a team, and to have excellent oral and written communication skills.

Salary: $50,000 to more than $100,000 a year

Moblogging

John Legend has more than one hundred videos on his Web site, documenting his life on the road, in the studio, and during interviews. These clips reflect a trend in using video as part of a Web site diary or a video blog. The term "moblog" was created as a conjunction of "mobile" and "blog" in order to describe a blog that features content from a mobile phone, either in still or video form. Mobloggers can upload their content to a wide variety of Internet sites, or they can create a Web site specific to their content. This can be done by creating a series of pages on a video-sharing site, such as YouTube; on a social-networking site, such as MySpace; or on a personal Web site.

Adrian Neylan, a cab driver in Sydney, Australia, has been blogging about his life since 2004. His site includes stories about various fares he has had, accidents he has witnessed, and other slices of Sydney life. In 2007 he started a moblog that includes videos created from his mobile phone, and the Australian Web site ninemsn.com.au installed additional cameras in his cab to help Neylan record the political opinions of average Sydney citizens during the 2007 national elections.

A wide variety of moblogs arose during the 2004 presidential election in the United States. Mobile phone provider Cingular provided journalism students from Columbia University and the University of California, Berkeley with video-capable phones and sent them to the national political conventions in Boston, Massachusetts and New York, New York. During the 2008 campaign, correspondents from washingtonpost.com and newsweek.com provided live video coverage via mobile phones. A variety of amateur mobloggers also covered the campaign and the election from a wide range of perspectives.

However, some mobile phone users create videos to record less appropriate, and sometimes illegal, activities. One example of this is related to the phenomenon called happy slapping.

A French youth throws a projectile into a crowd while his friend videotapes the incident with his cell phone during an occurance of happy slapping.

Happy Slapping

In several countries in Europe over the last few years, the general public has been introduced to a disturbing practice called happy slapping. Happy slapping is an outgrowth of bullying in general, but is not restricted to attacks on young people. One youth described it this way: "You see someone just sitting

Deleted but not Forever

Many users of personal electronics, including computers, digital cameras, and cell phones, believe that if a file is deleted, it is irretrievable. In fact, in many cases, the data is merely moved to another part of a hard drive, or broken into segments, making it possible for forensic electronics experts to recover the information for later study.

This fact of electronic life was demonstrated during an assault case involving members of the University of Minnesota football team. In April 2007 four players were attending a party in which one of the men and a female guest allegedly engaged in a drinking contest. According to court documents, the woman consumed eight shots of vodka, which rendered her extremely intoxicated and caused her to pass out. At some point after the drinking contest, one of the football players sexually assaulted the woman while one of the others filmed it with his cell phone camera.

The video was later deleted from the phone, but forensic experts were able to recover it. The electronic evidence, along with DNA evidence, resulted in the player's arrest on charges of criminal sexual conduct.

there, they look like they're dumb. You just run up to them and slap them. And run off. It's funny."[60] In addition, the assault is filmed using a mobile phone camera; some of the videos are sent to other phones and others are posted on the Internet.

In Great Britain, many of the attacks gained nationwide attention. The practice received widespread coverage in 2005 when a sixteen-year-old girl was beaten so badly that she suffered temporary blindness. Since then, other cases have involved both single-slap attacks and multiple-blow assaults, and some of these assaults involved more than one attacker. For example, four British teens filmed themselves approaching and attacking a stranger as he sat at a bus stop one early July morning in 2007. They left the forty-year-old man for dead, but he survived, albeit with multiple head injuries that initially required a six-hour brain operation.

The four youths were traced through text messages they sent to each other after the attack received media attention. Following a trial in May 2008, all four were sentenced to jail, with the seventeen-year-old ringleader convicted of attempted murder.

Happy slap attacks have been reported in other countries, including France, Germany, Spain, Denmark, Sweden, and Australia. A number of countries have enacted legislation making such behavior subject to prosecution, including the individual using the mobile phone to film the attack. But for sociologists, behaviorists, and victims' rights advocates, the motivations for these attacks remain unclear and debatable.

Does One Violent Video Encourage Another?

Happy slapping, and violent acts in general, that are recorded with cell phone cameras are subject to debate among scientists. Some believe that such reality television shows as *Jackass,* in which individuals deliberately subject each other to potentially painful stunts, are at the root of the phenomenon. Graham Barfield, a media lecturer at the University of East London, believes the individuals perpetrating the happy slap attacks envision their own videos as shortcuts to fame and notoriety among those who see the images online. He says, "What we see is kids watching these shows and thinking, 'Well, maybe I could stage my own scenes of pain and humiliation along these lines.'"[61]

Others theorize that, once one or more attacks on strangers have been released on the Internet or shown in the mainstream media, they take on lives of their own and become motivating factors. Maricelle Ruiz, director of the Web site Internet Business Law Services, writes, "In Spain, a friend of upper middle-class youths, who killed a homeless woman in a Barcelona ATM, says they had previously shown others aggressions against homeless individuals, recorded on mobile phones."[62]

BITS & BYTES

1.2 billion

Number of mobile phone users worldwide who use their phones to access the Internet

The Web on Your Phone

The interconnected nature of today's technology has led developers to examine ways to allow mobile phone users to experience the World Wide Web on their phones. The challenge was to render the language of the Web (called hypertext markup language, or HTML) for the relatively small screen while dealing with the memory capacity of the average cell phone.

Not only can cell phones users search the Web with their phones, they can do online banking, send e-mails, and do almost anything online they can do using a computer.

A Japanese innovation called i-mode succeeded in bringing the Web to mobile users. The technique is based on a compact version of HTML. This language was included in several early phone models and networks from 2002 to 2004, and served as many users' introduction to Web browsing on their phones.

Today, the i-mode application is widespread in Japan and Asia and is spreading into Europe. Other users around the world, including those in North America, access the Web via wireless access protocol (or WAP). Regardless of the method, increased speed of cellular networks and increased memory of cellular devices have led to greater access to Internet content from mobile phones. Both of these applications integrate the cell phone with Web-based browsers and pages.

Today, mobile phone users can do almost anything online that they can do using a computer. Business travelers can check the weather at their next destination; food enthusiasts can find directions to a new restaurant; students can access online reading assignments and submit assignments via e-mail. However, some users have taken advantage of the integration of mobile and Web in order to gain unfair advantages.

Mobile Phone Cheating

It seems that as long as instructors have been giving tests to students, some students have found ways to cheat. Nancy Stanlick, a philosophy professor at the University of Central Florida who hosts academic honesty seminars, has been teaching for more than twenty-five years. Over the years, she says she has seen methods of cheating come and go, and attitudes change toward it. Given today's technology, she says, "The temptations are there. The methods are only different."[63]

While undoubtedly the vast majority of students use their mobile phones for socializing and for keeping in touch with their families, some students around the world have chosen to use their cell phones to cheat. Some use their phones to SMS each other during tests to solicit answers. Others use their Web-enabled phones to surf the Internet for the answers and send the answers back to the participants while the exam is in progress. According to James E. Katz, chair of the Department of Communication at Rutgers University, at least one educator found a way to strike back at those who were cheating:

> A University of Maryland professor posted a bogus answer key on the Internet after a test had begun. By comparing students' answers with the bogus answer key, the teacher uncovered a dozen cheaters, who appeared to have independently had friends send them answers from the key.[64]

The proliferation of mobile phones among students across the world has led to educational institutions making difficult choices about cell phone use. Some school systems have banned the use of cell phones in classrooms, especially during exams. Some colleges and universities have developed special rooms for exams that are shielded from electronic signals. Stanlick believes such methods only address part of the problem. She says that while she has seen a rise in the number of

Camera Phones in the Classroom

Since the arrival of cell phone cameras, students around the world have been using them to take photos of their classmates, school outings, sports teams, and extracurricular activities. However, some students also have used their camera phones to take photos of tests or homework answers, in order to provide them to classmates, and others have created Web pages featuring photos of classmates or instructors that include fictional descriptions of the individuals' hobbies or behaviors.

Consequently, many school districts have banned the use of cell phones in the classroom, requiring that all phones are turned off during class. Others take more hands-on methods to ensure that the devices are not used inappropriately; for example, in schools in Great Falls, Montana, educators collect the students' phones at the beginning of class and return them when class is over.

students trying to sneak peeks at cell phones, she believes that the tools for cheating should not be blamed, but the attitudes that foster cheating in the first place. To this end, some schools rely on an honor system regarding cheating and believe that the students' belief in and adherence to the school's system will keep them from using their mobile phones to cheat.

Mobile Television

While some students might be using their cell phones to cheat others may be trying to watch television. People in Japan, China, South Korea, and Germany watch TV on their mobile phones every day. Cellular networks offer free streaming video of TV shows that millions enjoy daily. In the United States, however, there are far fewer viewers. The reason for this is three-fold: network speed, the type of TV signal being used, and price.

Cellular network speeds in the United States vary from carrier to carrier. The emerging third-generation (3G) standard for speed and data capability is more widespread in some areas of the world, such as Japan, and on some cellular providers in the United States. Most mobile phones sold today in the United States are 3G ready; the challenge is to ensure that the owner of a 3G handset is receiving 3G services.

The type of TV signal used in the United States is analog. This standard, however, is scheduled to change to digital in 2009. Understandably, cellular network providers have been reluctant to market any cell phones that could receive streaming video of analog broadcasts, because the phones will become obsolete when the digital changeover occurs. TV on mobile phones is more popular in Japan because Japanese TV broadcasts are already digital. Chinese TV will remain analog until 2015, and Germany created digital broadcast standards later than the United States, which enabled them to anticipate the growth of digital cellular technology.

The final stumbling block in opening the U.S. market to TV on cell phones has been the price. Many carriers charged a monthly fee for such service. In the eyes of John Barrett, research director at the analysis firm Parks Associates, charging fees makes a difference. He recommends that the networks provide free content, noting, "A free taste would go a long way in making the consumer case for mobile TV. Mobile TV services have taken off in Japan and South Korea, where service is offered free of charge. In Italy, where additional fees have been the norm, usage has been limited."[65]

Changes in Broadcasting

However, developments in early 2009 may herald a change in the market. Television stations in twenty-two American cities announced that by the end of 2009, they would begin broadcasting their signals in a format designed for viewing on portable devices. The stations represented affiliates of the ABC, CBS, Fox, NBC, CW, ION, and PBS networks, and are based in markets such as Chicago, New York, Philadelphia, San Francisco, and Boston.

This new technology uses a system that differs from the current setup offered by U.S. fee-based plans, and currently no devices available in the United States are capable of interpreting its signal. But part of the appeal of this technology will be the ability for mobile phone users to view local news, which is currently unavailable through fee-based plans.

The broadcasters feel that this new technology will spur manufacturers to create new devices for U.S. markets. Mobile telecommunications engineer and media consultant Tomi T. Ahonen recalls that when mobile TV was launched in Europe in 2001 with thirty-second summaries of the daily news, the same situation existed. He writes,

> There was exactly one phone model in the world that had the color screen and a powerful enough CPU to handle the tiny video clip—this was the brand new Nokia 9210 Communicator (the first [with a] color [screen])—and to watch a 30 second clip, would take about 2 minutes for the grainy poor quality and lousy sound clip to download over the fastest cellular technology of that time.[66]

Since that time, manufacturers have developed more innovations and cellular providers have upgraded their networks to meet consumer demand in Europe and Asia.

While the prospect of free TV on American mobile phones remains clouded, U.S. mobile phone operators and

users are exploring and expanding other technologies that already exist in other parts of the world. These include online banking and payment capabilities.

Paying by Cell Phone

Being able to access the Web via a mobile phone

In Japan a women demonstrates paying her railway fare with her cell phone. The Bay Area Rapid Transit (BART) in California is testing a similar use of cell phones to pay for subway fares.

has led to a variety of applications that were little imagined just a few years ago. Integrated banking applications in countries such as the Philippines and South Africa enable employees to receive their paychecks via SMS. Across the world, cell phones with wireless chips inside act as debit cards for a wide variety of purchases. For example, all parking meters in Estonia are SMS enabled. Drivers text the meter's code to have the parking fee deducted from their bank account. In Helsinki, Finland, 60 percent of all single tickets sold for the public transportation system are paid for by SMS. Mobile phone users visit a ticket kiosk and text a particular code to a phone number on the kiosk; the rider is charged the ticket price as the machine dispenses the ticket.

In San Francisco, California, the Bay Area Rapid Transit (or BART) system is testing the ability to pay for subway fares with cell phones. These phones are equipped with near-field communications (NFC) technology, a system that receives and transmits a very low power radio signal and the same technology that is found in smart cards. Users who have NFC-equipped phones run them over NFC scanners in the turnstiles, and the commuter's prepaid account is debited the appropriate fare. Journalist Ryan Kim says that BART director James Fang sees great potential in the technology. In the *San Francisco Chronicle* newspaper Kim writes,

> If the BART trial goes well, Fang said the same chip used by BART riders could be linked with other smart-card supporting retailers and transit agencies. Fang said the

phone payment service could also provide an environmental boost for BART, helping it trim the amount of paper it uses for tickets. BART currently creates 32 million tickets a year.[67]

The developers of the technology say the phone payments are both convenient and secure. The cell phone user has to open the payment program on his or her phone, which will enable payments only for the next two minutes. And, as an added security precaution, the application is preprogrammed with a $48 limit to minimize any losses due to theft.

For millions of users around the world, paying for purchases with their mobile phones is now second nature. For millions more, the technology will soon be available, as banks and cellular networks work to integrate electronic payments for their customers. The key for all is to use systems that ensure privacy and security while ensuring the accuracy of each transaction. This is yet another example of how mobile phone technology is reshaping the way the world lives.

Reshaping the World of Communications

Clearly the proliferation of the mobile phone has enabled users around the world to perform a multitude of tasks that the originators of the device could not have imagined. The integration of still and video cameras has helped mobile phone users document everything from birthdays to bombings and holidays to hurricanes. The development of the Internet-capable cell phone has enabled users to have the World Wide Web at their fingertips at all times. And the convergence of mobile phones and wireless payments has streamlined money matters for millions.

As the twenty-first century unfolds, mobile phone developers continue to create innovative technologies as they work to create the next generations of services and devices. These men and women dream of new ways to integrate the phone into daily life, to make everyday tasks easier, and to enable the devices to perform tasks previously unimagined. Considering how far the mobile phone has come just since the year 2000, it is not hard to imagine that more advances lie ahead.

CHAPTER 5

The Future of Phoning

Cellular phones have become an integral part of the lives of billions of people around the world. They use them to make and receive calls away from their homes, businesses, or schools—the original reason that mobile phones were invented. It allows them to stay in contact while on the go. They can stay in touch with friends and family wirelessly, without having to use a traditional phone for calling or a computer to send e-mail. Today, the cell phone has expanded to incorporate other means of communication and various tools. They are used to send and receive text messages, to take and share pictures and videos, and to keep track of contact information for their friends and family.

Because the uses and impacts of cell phones were underestimated in the beginning, even within the mobile phone community, many marketing experts, sociologists, and cell phone technology developers are often reluctant to make predictions about where mobile phones are headed in the future. Almost every technology has enthusiasts who predict radical advances that will change the world. But few such enthusiasts anticipated the widespread acceptance of the cell phone, much less its increasing versatility. Consequently, any prediction for mobile phone development must be seen as just that—a prediction.

The New Home Phone?

Some studies suggest that the cell phone may become the future home phone, as mobile phone users are opting to make their cell phone their only phone. A December 2008 survey by the Centers for Disease Control and Prevention found that 17.5 percent of all U.S. households used only cell phones. However, the numbers are higher for younger consumers; nearly 36 percent of adults ages twenty-five to twenty-nine live in households without traditional phones. Additionally, 63 percent of adults living with unrelated roommates live in wireless-only homes. Clearly more Americans are choosing to disconnect from the network of landline telephones, preferring to make all their calls from a mobile phone.

Some consumers still own a landline and do not feel the need to go completely wireless with their phone line yet.

Mobile users who rely on their cell phone as a means of keeping in touch often find themselves faced with a dilemma. They have given their mobile number out to all their friends and family, and they get the majority of their calls through the cell. The traditional phone—the landline—remains little used, if at all.

Many consumers are choosing to disconnect from the landline network, opting to consolidate their phoning into just one service. They cite many benefits of the choice, including saving money; they only have to pay for one service instead of two. Wireless advocates maintain that for the cost of basic wireless service, a consumer can have all the benefits of a landline. Ed Forman, owner of Express Wireless in Topeka, Kansas, sells products for Verizon Wireless. He says, "When they're having two devices already, your average cost on a home line is anywhere from $43 to $65 a month to having a cellular service that can be as low as $39 a month, allowing you the same freedom and having the free nationwide long distance."[68]

However, those who choose to keep a landline refer to several advantages to staying wired. Landline calling plans come with a variety of options; a consumer may choose to keep the landline connected purely for local service, or for home business equipment, such as a fax machine or a home security system. These consumers may own and use a cell phone, but for the present and foreseeable future, they choose not to go completely wireless.

Another consideration for consumers is the reliability of electricity in their community. Consumer expert Herb Weisbaum says, "I like the security a landline gives me in case of an emergency, such as a power outage."[69] While rare outages can be a nuisance, repeated outages may lead to more problems for those who rely on cell phones. A localized power outage may mean that a family's cell phones do not get recharged, leaving the phones unusable. A more widespread power outage may disable the electrical supply to the area's cell phone towers, leaving cellular customers without service. For example, severe weather and high winds in Michigan on December 28, 2008, caused power outages to AT&T's wireless system, leaving wireless consumers from Chicago, Illinois, to Detroit, Michigan, without service for almost the entire day.

For most consumers, the choice comes down to a matter of preference. But important safety considerations need to be taken into account. Despite increased cell coverage across the globe, cell phones still have a disadvantage over landlines in the United States: access to 911 emergency services.

Emergency Situations

Over the past ten years, the expansion of cellular coverage across the United States means cell phone users are less often out of touch, even in areas that were once considered remote. However, even in large cities, a call to 911 from a cell phone can delay emergency responses. Consequently, a mobile phone may not be the ideal means to report an emergency. For example, an emergency call from a landline phone in an apartment on the twentieth floor of an apartment building will give responders the street address and the apartment number. At best, a cell phone will give emergency operators the building's address. Steve Marzolf of the

Missing for Nine Days

In the late fall of 2006, James Kim, his wife Kati, and their two young daughters, Penelope and Sabine, left their home in San Francisco, California, by car for a Thanksgiving holiday trip to the Pacific Northwest. When the family did not show up for appointments on November 28, friends and coworkers became concerned. The family was known for keeping in touch by cell phone or e-mail.

Using their last known location, a restaurant in southwestern Oregon, searchers began looking for the family's car. Cellular phone network employees reported that a tower in the rugged terrain of Josephine County had received a signal from one of the family's cell phones, which directed searchers to a new area. On December 4, Kati and the girls were found alive by rescuers in the car; the car had become stuck in the snow on a road at an elevation of 3,500 feet (1,067m). They had been missing for nine days, surviving with the few food supplies they had in the car.

James Kim's body was found on December 6. He had left his family to find help on December 2, two days before the rescuers arrived. Rescuers credit the fleeting moments when the family's cell phone signal reached the remote tower as a major factor in the survivors' rescue.

National Association of State 911 Administrators says, "So even if we nail your location, we don't know what floor you are on. That's a real problem if you're having a heart attack and we need to find you in a hurry."[70]

The Federal Communications Commission (FCC) reported in October 2008 that public safety officials estimate that fully 50 percent of calls to 911 are coming from mobile phones, and that the number is growing annually. Current FCC regulations require all cell phone providers to forward emergency calls to a public safety call center, whether the caller is a subscriber or not. The network must provide the caller's location, within 164 to 984 feet (50m to 300m), but that can be a large margin of error in emergency situations.

In response, the FCC set regulations in 2007 requiring more precise location information, and network providers have five years to comply with the new requirement. Consequently, network providers are working to meet the target date. One way they are doing so is through enhanced GPS information.

Smartphones, like the one pictured here, contain GPS and allow users to be rescued if they are ever lost or in need of help.

Enhanced GPS

GPS (Global Positioning System) is a satellite-based system that allows users to pinpoint their location almost anywhere on Earth. A GPS unit sends a signal that, ideally, bounces off three satellites, providing the device with three latitude and longitude measurements. The unit then uses that data to triangulate the user's location. It has been an invaluable tool to help rescuers to find lost individuals.

Mobile phones sold in the United States today contain GPS capability. Following the terrorist attacks on the United States on September 11, 2001, U.S. cell phone manufacturers were mandated by the federal government to develop and sell models with GPS technology within five years. The technology enables network providers to pinpoint the caller's location when they call 911. In many mobile phones, that is all the GPS technology can do.

However, a new generation of handheld devices is enabling 911 operators to assist callers more accurately, even in remote areas. Devices called smartphones marry a variety of cell phone functions with new technologies, such as GPS-based mapping services. Popular smartphones offering the service include Apple's iPhone 3G and a variety of models from RIM, the manufacturer of the BlackBerry line of mobiles.

Until recently, the ability to map one's location and route using GPS technology was only available through handheld GPS receivers, which are popular with backcountry enthusiasts, and through in-vehicle devices, called satnavs. Popular satnav devices by Garmin and TomTom provide maps, street addresses, and driving directions. But smartphones enable the user to do more with GPS technology than receive maps and driving directions. These devices enable the user to make a call or send a message that he or she is lost, delayed, or in need of help.

Consequently, smartphones are beginning to outsell satnavs in many parts of the world, such as Europe and the

Middle East. Chris Jones is vice president and chief analyst of the high-tech industry analysis firm Canalys. He says while sales of satnavs in North America remained strong in 2008, the future may be less rosy due to the growing popularity of smartphones. Jones notes that "with GPS being built into the majority of smartphones, and users increasingly being given maps on their phone by default, and multiple reasons to use them, the threat to [satnav] vendors is rising quickly... smartphone vendors are learning and releasing new devices and software all the time."[71]

Your Location—On Demand

Other tech experts foresee additional capabilities once a user's location is determined. *Computerworld* magazine's Mike Elgan predicted in November 2008 that by 2012, the mobile phone will be automatically linked to the user's social networking applications, such as Facebook or MySpace. He says, "Your cell phone will use multiple technologies, such as GPS, tower triangulation, and Wi-Fi network identification to constantly pinpoint your location. Social networking tools will always tell you when friends are near and always give you location-relevant search results, weather reports, and real-time data."[72]

This integration may provide the next logical step in being able to know where friends and family are at all times. Each family member could be viewed on a mobile map as they travel around town. The future may lie in the integration with mapping and imaging technologies, such as Street View. This feature of the Google Maps Web site merges traditional street maps with street-level views taken from 360-degree cameras mounted atop vehicles that drive through cities around the world. Such a feature could enable future mobile phone users to share the same visual perspective as a friend behind the wheel driving around town or while on vacation in a foreign city.

Advances in Design

The evolution of the mobile phone since the 1980s is perhaps unrivaled by any piece of technology, with the possible exception of the personal computer. Both have undergone radical changes in design and capabilities, as advances in microprocessor technology have contributed to greater computing power. For example, Intel Corporation's Core 2 Duo processes information up to fifteen thousand times faster than a chip they introduced thirty years earlier. Coupled with this increased speed are advances in miniaturization. Modern chips measure less than 1 inch (2.2cm) on each side.

As cell phone developers took advantage of these breakthroughs, mobiles have become smaller and more powerful. This in turn has led to enhanced features and innovative designs. Most of these are recognized only within the community of mobile enthusiasts. But one product debut in 2007 was heralded as revolutionary by both enthusiasts and the general public alike.

Enter the iPhone

One of the most famous examples of a revolution in design came with the introduction of Apple's iPhone in early 2007. This GSM smartphone features a compact size; a high-resolution, full-color screen almost as big as the unit itself; a built-in iPod music player; touch-screen functions for navigating menus; and an on-screen keyboard. Unprecedented publicity led to heavy demand. When it went on sale in the United States in June, some stores sold out within hours. Apple stores sold an estimated 128,000 iPhones on the first day; Apple's telecommunications partner, AT&T, sold an estimated 78,000 in the same period.

Many observers, both inside and outside the mobile phone industry, heralded Apple's entry into the cellular phone market. Citing the company's history of innovation and user-friendly features in personal computing and portable music players, critics and consumers thought that the iPhone would be a hit. Certainly its sleek design, uncluttered by buttons and keys, seemed simple and elegant and added to its appeal.

The iPhone's beautiful design, intuitive user's menu, and touch-screen technology that reacted to finger touches, sweeps, and flicks won raves from both users and critics. It received a variety of awards in 2008, including the prestigious Black Pencil Award for achievement in product design from

WIRELESS SUBSCRIBERS IN THE UNITED STATES (1995-2008)

	June 2008	June 2005	June 2000	June 1995
Number of Wireless Subscribers	262.7 Million	194.4 Million	97 Million	28.1 Million
Percent of Total U.S. Population	84%	66%	34%	11%

Taken from: data from CTIA. Available online at
http://www.ctia.org/advocacy/research/index.cfm/AID/10323

D&AD, an educational charity that recognizes excellence in design and creativity. However, its hardware left some critics less than impressed. The original 2G model had just 4 gigabytes of memory. Touch-screen technology had been available on an award-winning model from the company LG in 2006. The Nokia 9300i had a larger screen. The iPhone's camera offered lower resolution than many other camera phones on the market, and it had no video recording capabilities. Additionally, many SMS enthusiasts and mobile marketing experts felt the touch screen forced the user to SMS using both hands, unlike phones with traditional keypads.

Nevertheless, mobile marketing experts acknowledged that it was a hit with consumers. For example, the advanced iPhone 3G, with 8 gigabytes of memory, won the Phone of the Year Award for 2008 from Great Britain's *What Mobile* magazine. It has become an extremely familiar model in a field of hundreds of other mobiles, and it serves as an example of how far mobile innovation and design have come in less than forty years.

As a way of measuring these advances, compare the first commercially available model, Motorola's DynaTAC 8000X, to the iPhone. The DynaTAC weighed close to 2 pounds (907g), and measured 13 inches tall by 1.75 inches wide by 3.5 inches deep (33cm by 4.4cm by 8.6cm). The iPhone 3G weighs 4.7 ounces (133g), and measures 4.5 inches by 2.4 inches by 0.46 inches deep (11.4cm by 6.0cm by 1.2cm). The DynaTAC cost close to $4,000 in 1983; the iPhone today costs as little as $99.

Competition Leads to Variety

Consumers do not need to buy an iPhone to take advantage of advances in design and power. Complex chip sets and advanced electronics offer amazing speed, full-color graphics, and light weight in even inexpensive mobile phones. For example, a cell phone that debuted in October 2008 had a slide-out QWERTY keyboard, expandable memory up to 16 gigabytes, stereo sound, and a camera with the ability to capture images with a 2-megapixel resolution. The phone's suggested retail price was $50.

The competition among cellular phone manufacturers and network providers remains fierce. Within a year of the release of the iPhone 3G, several manufacturers offered phones with similar capabilities for a lower price than Apple's device, or with more advanced features for a similar price. For example, the Samsung Omnia offers a 5-megapixel camera for roughly the same price as the iPhone which has a 2-megapixel unit.

As consumers navigate the maze of competing devices, features, and networks, cellular companies are working to develop the next generations of connectivity. The changes from 1G devices and networks to 2G digitization were clear-cut; a device and a network were either digital or not. However, the advances beyond 2G are murkier waters.

Going Beyond 3G

In 2008 and 2009 competing cellular providers in the United States heavily advertised their networks' third-generation (3G) network capabilities. Consumers had to navigate competing claims about coverage and download speeds. However, what designates a 3G network is subject to debate. As 2G technology was being rolled out, developers debated 3G's targets for speed and data transfer. No internationally accepted standards for 3G were ever decided. Consequently, 3G providers can deliver speeds as fast as 2 megabits per second or as low as 384 kilobits per second and still call their service 3G.

Even as the cellular networks strive to get customers signed up for their 3G services, technology developers are contemplating the next generation of cellular technology, which is being called 4G. The greatest advance in 4G may be the ability for networks to accommodate more calls, as well as demands for mobile video, Internet access, SMS, and multimedia messaging services. While no standards have yet been set for 4G, telecommunications companies around the world are shooting for speeds between 100 megabits per second (Mbps) and 1 gigabit per second. However, 4G networks that exist in cities around the world tend to offer speeds of 3 to 5 Mbps. For example, a network in seven cities in Denmark offers rates as low as $10.00 per month for 4 Mbps service. While that is significantly slower than 4G targets, it is still approximately three times faster than many 3G networks found in the United States.

In places like South Korea and Japan, 4G networks enable mobile phone users to watch television and videos on their handhelds. In the United States, however, 4G service is currently only available in Portland, Oregon, and in Baltimore, Maryland, through a wireless data system called WiMax. *Computerworld*'s Brian Nadel says, "Think about receiving the equivalent of a home DSL or cable broadband connection while you're mobile, and you get an idea of its potential to put data everywhere you'll be. In other words, WiMax can turn a city into a hot spot for wireless data."[73]

Sending Multimedia Messages

The coming 4G technology promises greater speeds for data transfer. These speeds would be a boon to a number of technologies that currently exist but are little used. One of these is multimedia messaging service (MMS), which allows mobile phone videos to be directly encoded into an e-mail or a text message, so that no attachments are necessary.

MMS is an outgrowth of SMS, but has not proven as popular with consumers. Technology experts suggest that one drawback is with handset technology. Currently, sending an MMS message requires the mobile phone user to set several parameters within the phone's system, which may deter some users due to the complexity involved. However, changes in device systems and software may move MMS forward, and its future may lie in the implementation of 4G networks.

New Obsolescence

In a consumer-driven society, manufacturers are constantly working to develop new products to bring to market. The

Sometimes the number of models of mobile phones available to consumers can be overwhelming.

cellular telephone industry is no different than any other. But unlike other technology products, such as cameras or personal computers, mobile phones generally come with a contract for service. The customer agrees to use the provider's service for a set period of time (in the United States, usually eighteen months to two years) and may be subject to monetary penalties if the contract is broken. As a result, most consumers keep their phones for at least the term of their contract.

When the contract expires, many consumers start shopping for a new plan. They may be looking to upgrade their service or change networks or are intrigued by an offer that may save them money. But a visit to a mobile phone provider's store may result in an overabundance of choices, as new models seem to be introduced every week, with new colors, with more memory, and with new accessories. Consequently, some consumers feel that a new phone is their only option in order to stay current with the technology.

Cellular providers often offer a free phone with a new contract. Sometimes more than one free phone is part of the deal, enticing consumers to ensure that all family members have phones. These new cell phones may replace older ones that function perfectly well, but are now deemed obsolete by the carrier because the plan attached to them has expired or by the consumer because they are not the most current model.

Although this practice of planned obsolescence is not confined to the cell phone industry, many consumers are unprepared for it. Often, they struggle with what to do with the older phones. Some donate them to charities; others simply throw them in the trash. Both practices can be dangerous. Phones that are donated may still have personal information in the memory, such as names and addresses, which may expose the former owner to identity theft. Phones that are discarded outright pose

Cell Phone Disposal and Recycling

Each year, more than 125 million cell phones are thrown away, ending up in landfills around the world. Each phone contains hazardous materials, including cadmium and antimony, as well as valuable metals, such as copper, gold, and silver. These metals can pollute the ground water surrounding the landfill.

Fortunately, there are a variety of ways to recycle cell phones. For example, Sprint will accept customers' old phones and accessories through its Project Connect program, in which phones are recycled or resold. A charity called Cell Phones for Soldiers collects old mobiles and sells them to recycling companies. The money it receives from the sales is used to purchase prepaid calling cards for U.S. troops overseas.

Phones that are no longer usable can be recycled for their resources. Thierry Van Kerckhoven is a manager at Umicore, a Belgian company that began as a mining company in the 1800s. Today Umicore uses its smelting and refining technology to reclaim the metals in cell phones. The metals can then be reused in electronics or jewelry. In the online video "The Secret Life of Cell Phones" by Inform, a nonprofit advocacy group, Van Kerckhoven says, "If we recycle one [metric ton, or 2,200 lbs.] of cell phones, we will recover more than 3.5 kg of silver."

a wide variety of environmental problems. Hazards from these handsets include groundwater contamination from aging and leaking batteries and from nonbiodegradable metals and plastics. With 1.1 billion new phones purchased worldwide in 2008 alone, environmentalists are concerned about the millions of mobiles that are just being thrown away.

Concerns about the environmental impact of discarded cell phones are not unique. Environmental awareness over the years has encompassed discarded items from aluminum cans to washing machines, leading to community efforts to reduce the amount of recyclable items placed in landfills. As more retailers accept old phones for recycling, consumers may be encouraged to turn in their old phones when purchasing a new one.

Open Software

The possibilities of evolving wireless technology seem endless, but some short-term predictions have come true, such as the arrival of open-source operating systems. These systems enable the user to reprogram and modify cell phone software for enhanced personalization. According to journalist Brian Bergstein, being able to customize one's mobile phone with any number of new programs "would have seemed like a stretch until recently, when the idea began to take hold that cell phones should be as open to new programs as PCs are to Web sites."[74]

For example, in the spring of 2008, a class of Massachusetts Institute of Technology computer technology students was asked to come up with new applications for cell phones. Anticipating the arrival of Google's Android cell phone operating system, which can be reprogrammed by each user, Hal Abelson challenged the students to develop programs that could run on Android. One of the programs they created allowed users to configure their phones to automatically switch to vibrate mode in the office or silent mode in the library or movie theater. Another program gave users a way to use to-do lists and reminders to better advantage; if a to-do list includes "buy milk," the program sends a prompting text and buzzes when the consumer passes a grocery store. Less than six months later, in October 2008, the first Android-powered mobile, the T-Mobile G1, hit the market. More Android-powered models are expected by the end of 2009.

New Hybrid Devices

Another innovation, already in the test phase, could save lives around the world. University of California, Berkeley bioengineer professor Daniel Fletcher and his students created an all-in-one camera phone–microscope called the CellScope, a device that takes photographs up to fifty times magnification, which is enough to see red blood cells in a sample. Tests of the device in Africa have yielded amazing results. One of Fletcher's students worked with doctors in remote areas of the Democratic Republic of the Congo. They photographed blood samples of patients and e-mailed them to labs for diagnoses of such diseases as malaria and sickle-cell anemia. Malaria-infected blood samples show parasites inside red blood cells; blood samples of sickle cell–infected patients show abnormal red blood cells that are bent in the shape of a C.

At the moment, the CellScope looks like a cell phone with a kaleidoscope attached. Its design is likely to change with advanced optics, miniaturization, and materials. Each of these areas also is being used in concepts and prototypes that developers are imagining for the mobiles of tomorrow.

The Shape of Things to Come

A bellwether for the coming year in technology is the annual Consumer Electronics Show. Among the mobile phones at the 2009 show was Palm's new smartphone, called the Pre, which was touted by one technology critic as "a match for the Apple iPhone. Perhaps more than a match."[75] Several features, including a 3-megapixel camera with a flash, a touch screen, and a slide-down QWERTY keyboard, helped make the Pre a hit at the show. LG unveiled a phone called the GD910 3G, which combines a touch screen, stereo sound, a speakerphone, and a music player, and it is worn on the wrist. In June 2009, LG announced it would be available for sale in Europe in July, and around the world by the end of the year.

Although the GD910 has a traditional watchband, engineers are already envisioning phones that can be molded to fit your wrist or folded to fit anywhere. In February 2008, a partnership between Nokia and Great Britain's University of Cambridge unveiled the Morph, which they call "a concept that demonstrates how future mobile devices might be stretchable and flexible, allowing the user to transform their mobile device into radically different shapes."[76] The device takes advantage of nanotechnology (which studies and controls matter at the atomic level), and the partnership envisions some of Morph's features being integrated into high-end cell phones by 2015.

Clearly, a transparent and foldable mobile phone is just a concept at present. But the integration of the cell phone and cutting-edge (and as yet theoretical) materials demonstrates that developers believe that mobiles today are an ever-increasing integral part of our world. A foldable phone may not be within the reach of everyone when, or if, it reaches the consumer market. But manufacturers are not restricting themselves to such concept models developed in laboratories.

A Fully Interconnected World

Many manufacturers have representatives traveling the globe to see how cell phones can make life easier in remote corners of the world. They examine the special problems posed by these areas, such as intermittent electrical supplies, distances to cell phone towers, and the expense of devices. They talk to people who have mobiles and those who do not, asking about how they see cell phones and about what features they would like. For some, the phone should be waterproof, so it could be used during the monsoon season. For others, it should have a way of charging it without dependence on the electric grid, like a self-winding watch or hand-cranked flashlight.

Already, the mobile phone is responsible for changing the way people around the world conduct their personal and professional lives. In developed countries, people use them to call clients when they are running late and to call family to let them know they are on the way home. But now, in developing countries, businesspeople are using them to grow their businesses, earn more money, and help their families, thus growing their nation's economy. For example, in Bangladesh, microloans have helped more than 250,000 women invest in specially designed cell phone kits with long-lasting batteries. The women set up shop in villages and neighborhoods and serve as the local phone operator, charging a small commission for people to make and receive calls.

Additionally, the mobile phone is responsible for changing the way people around the world interact. They share music, videos, and jokes; they e-mail pictures of friends, family, and pets; they hail cabs in Singapore and order pizza in Spokane; they SMS from everywhere. Millions worldwide participate via their phones by calling in or texting their vote for contestants on reality shows like *American Idol*. And some analysts contend that widespread use of SMS

This man is just one of milliions around the world phoning in his vote for the television show American Idol *using his cell phone. The mobile phone is responsible for changing the way people around the world interact.*

International Travel

The increasingly global nature of the world's economy and the ease of international travel mean many people travel overseas for business, pleasure, or education. In these circumstances, using a generic mobile may be impossible.

While the global system for mobile communications (GSM) is the standard in dozens of countries around the world, code division multiple access (CDMA) networks also are widespread. For example, an American with a CDMA phone will find CDMA service in Delhi, India, but not in Stuttgart, Germany.

One way to avoid such problems is to upgrade to an internationally compatible phone that can work on more than one digital network. This is particularly helpful if the traveler is going to more than one country. Most network providers have agreements with carriers overseas, which enable international calling. The traveler may need to purchase upgraded services to enable this feature, which costs extra. The overseas services may not include some options (such as texting) and international roaming rates may apply.

Other travelers, such as business people on assignment or students studying abroad, may wish to purchase a local phone and a local calling plan to make local calling in their new home cheaper.

during the 2008 U.S. presidential campaign contributed to Barack Obama's victory. All this has led one observer to label this new world as a "mobile society."

Our Mobile Society

In the 2008 U.S. presidential election, volunteers and staffers for both candidates worked to drum up support among voters and to ensure that individuals went to the polls. However, Barack Obama's campaign was more effective in its use of mobile phone technology. His supporters collected mobile phone numbers at events across the country. These citizens, in turn, were the first to learn of Obama's choice of running mate, which was announced by text message. By November, the campaign had collected six million cell phone numbers and each received a message on Election Day reminding them to vote. It was unprecedented in American politics and an effective and inexpensive way to get out the vote.

As Americans discover the power of the mobile phone and all its capabilities, they discover what millions of others around the world have already done. The mobile phone can be a wonderful technology for all aspects of life. Mobile telecommunications engineer and media consultant Alan Moore calls this worldwide transformation part of a move from an industrial society to a "mobile society." He says that because humans are social,

> we are programmed to be a "we species"—a social networking species with an innate need to connect and communicate.... That is why we are inevitably moving towards the Mobile Society, where our mobile devices become the remote control for our daily lives. Because any technology that allows us to better connect, communicate, share knowledge and information, and get stuff done will be widely adopted.... The Mobile Society will bring unprecedented flows of communication and these flows of information and communication are the engines of innovation and commerce.[77]

The cellular telephone has truly changed the way people stay in touch. They call to keep friends, family, and colleagues informed on where they are and what they are doing. They text to let their friends know what happened in school or on the way home. They use a cell phone to keep their lives organized, from saving phone numbers to managing their photographs and finances. They use them to listen to their favorite songs, to watch their favorite videos, and to surf the Web. Each cell phone reflects the personality of its owner. And as cell phone technology continues to evolve, the future may lie in enabling billions around the world to share common experiences and insights across the current divides of cultures and nationalities. This may be the promise of a truly mobile society.

NOTES

Chapter 1: The History of the Cellular Telephone

1. Tom Farley, "The Cell-Phone Revolution," *American Heritage Invention & Technology*, Winter 2007, www.americanheritage.com/events/articles/web/20070110-cell-phone-att-mobile-phone-motorola-federal-communications-commission-cdma-tdma-gsm.shtml.
2. SRI International, "The Role of NSF's Support of Engineering in Enabling Technological Innovation—Phase II," SRI International, May 1998, www.sri.com/policy/csted/reports/sandt/techin2/chp4.html.
3. Quoted in Farley, "The Cell-Phone Revolution."
4. Farley, "The Cell-Phone Revolution."
5. SRI International, "The Role of NSF's Support of Engineering in Enabling Technological Innovation—Phase II."
6. Gerard Goggin, *Cell Phone Culture: Mobile Technology in Everyday Life.* London: Routledge, 2006, pp. 30–31.
7. Tom Farley, "Mobile Telephone History," Privateline.com, April 9, 2006, www.telecomwriting.com/PCS/history9.htm.

Chapter 2: The Evolution of Mobile Phoning

8. Tom Farley, "Basic Wireless Principles: Channels," Privateline.com, http://privateline.com/PCS/channels.html.
9. Goggin, *Cell Phone Culture*, p. 31.
10. Nick Foggin, "Mythology and Mobile Data," in *Thumb Culture: The Meaning of Mobile Phones for Society*, eds. Peter Glotz, Stefan Bertschi, and Chris Locke. New Brunswick, NJ: Transaction, 2005, p. 251.
11. Richard Wray, "Half World's Population 'Will Have Mobile Phone by End of Year,'" guardian.co.uk, September 26, 2008, www.guardian.co.uk/technology/2008/sep/26/mobilephones.unitednations.
12. Quoted in Jim Butts, "Residents Fuming over Planned Cell Tower," *Northwest Herald*, September 25, 2008, http://nwherald.com/articles/2008/10/25/news/local/doc4902a739ddc47379119050.txt.
13. Quoted in Butts, "Residents Fuming over Planned Cell Tower."

14. Sasha Frere-Jones, "Ring My Bell: The Expensive Pleasures of the Ringtone," *New Yorker,* March 7, 2005, www.newyorker.com/archive/2005/03/07/050307crmu_music?currentPage=1.

15. Quoted in Frere-Jones, "Ring My Bell."

16. Quoted in Larissa Hjorth, "Postal Presence: A Case Study of Mobile Customization and Gender in Melbourne," in *Thumb Culture,* eds. Glotz, Bertschi, and Locke, p. 59.

17. Isabelle Leonard, personal correspondence, February 24, 2009.

18. Victoria Shannon, "Global Market for Cellphone Ring Tones Is Shrinking," *New York Times,* December 31, 2007, www.nytimes.com/2007/12/31/business/31ringtone.html?ex=1356757200&en=d527a627a5fd98e4&ei=5090&partner=rssuserland&emc=rss.

19. Christine Rosen, "Our Cell Phones, Ourselves," *New Atlantis,* Summer 2004, www.thenewatlantis.com/publications/our-cell-phones-ourselves.

20. Joachim R. Höflich, "The Mobile Phone and the Dynamic Between Private and Public Communication: Results of an International Exploratory Study," in *Thumb Culture,* eds. Glotz, Bertschi, and Locke, p. 125.

21. James E. Katz, *Magic in the Air: Mobile Communication and the Transformation of Social Life,* New Brunswick, NJ: Transaction, 2006, p. 23.

22. BBC News, "Europe Clears Mobiles on Aircraft," BBC News, April 7, 2008, http://news.bbc.co.uk/2/hi/technology/7334372.stm.

23. Hans Geser, "Is the Cell Phone Undermining the Social Order? Understanding Mobile Technology from a Sociological Perspective," in *Thumb Culture,* eds. Glotz, Bertschi, and Locke, p. 32.

24. Richard Ling, "Mobile Communication and Mediate Ritual," in *Communications in the 21st Century,* ed. K. Nyiri. Budapest, Hungary: 2007, www.richardling.com/papers/2007_Mobile_communication_and_mediated_ritual.pdf.

25. Ling, "Mobile Communication and Mediate Ritual."

26. Quoted in Jonathan Donner, "The Social and Economic Implications of Mobile Telephony in Rwanda," in *Thumb Culture,* eds. Glotz, Bertschi, and Locke, p. 46.

27. Genevieve Bell, "The Age of the Thumb: A Cultural Reading of Mobile Technologies from Asia," in *Thumb Culture,* eds. Glotz, Bertschi, and Locke, p. 75.

28. Quoted in Eric Weiner, "Our Cell Phones, Ourselves," National Public Radio, December 24, 2007, www.npr.org/templates/story/story.php?storyId=17486953.

Chapter 3: Text Messaging Goes Global

29. Tomi A. Ahonen, "Making Sense of the Biggest Data App on the Planet:

SMS Text Messaging," Communities Dominate Brands blog, July 13, 2006, http://communities-dominate.blogs.com/brands/2006/07/making_sense_of.html.

30. Victoria Shannon, "15 Years of Text Messages, a 'Cultural Phenomenon,'" *International Herald Tribune,* December 5, 2007, www.iht.com/articles/2007/12/05/technology/sms.php?page=1.

31. Bell, "The Age of the Thumb," p. 77.

32. Quoted in Goggin, *Cell Phone Culture,* p. 73.

33. Charles McGrath, "The Pleasures of the Text," *New York Times,* January 22, 2006, www.nytimes.com/2006/01/22/magazine/22wwln_lead.html?_r=1&oref=slogin.

34. Goggin, *Cell Phone Culture,* p. 75.

35. Goggin, *Cell Phone Culture,* p. 96.

36. Goggin, *Cell Phone Culture,* p. 96.

37. C. Tane Akamatsu, Connie Mayer, and Shona Farrelly, "An Investigation of Two-Way Text Messaging Use with Deaf Students at the Secondary Level," *Journal of Deaf Studies and Deaf Education,* Winter 2006, http://jdsde.oxfordjournals.org/cgi/reprint/11/1/120.

38. Akamatsu, Mayer, and Farrelly, "An Investigation of Two-Way Text Messaging Use with Deaf Students at the Secondary Level."

39. Quoted in Joachim R. Höflich and Julian Gebhardt, "Changing Cultures of Written Communication: Letter—E-mail—SMS," in *The Inside Text: Social, Cultural*

and Design Perspectives on SMS, eds. Richard Harper, Leysia Ann Paylen, and Alex Taylor. Norwell, MA: Springer, 2005, p. 20.

40. Richard Harper, "From Teenage Life to Victorian Morals and Back: Technological Change and Teenage Life," in *Thumb Culture,* eds. Glotz, Bertschi, and Locke, pp. 108–09.

41. Chana Joffe-Walt, "Three Generations' Views of Cell Phones," National Public Radio, December 25, 2007, www.npr.org/templates/story/story.php?storyId=17603266.

42. Quoted in Joel Garreau, "Textwalkers: Do They Need a Heads-Up?" *Washington Post,* August 25, 2008, www.washingtonpost.com/wpdyn/content/article/2008/08/24/AR2008082402275.html.

43. Quoted in Garreau, "Textwalkers."

44. Quoted in F. Hurley, "'Illiterate' Blast at Text Message Kids," *Sun,* March 3, 2003.

45. Quoted in Tim Barker, "Teens Say They Do a lot of Texting, but It's not Writing," *St. Louis Post-Dispatch,* April 25, 2008, www.stltoday.com/stltoday/news/stories.nsf/stlouiscitycounty/story/705DADED3523254C8625743600073DC7?OpenDocument.

46. Quoted in Barker, "Teens Say They Do a lot of Texting, but It's not Writing."

47. Quoted in Barker, "Teens Say They Do a lot of Texting, but It's not Writing."

48. Goggin, *Cell Phone Culture,* p. 115.

49. Quoted in JoNel Aliccia, "Texters Hurt as They Walk, Ride—Even Cook," MSNBC.com, July 30,

2008, www.msnbc.msn.com/id/ 25934644.

50. Quoted in Aliccia, "Texters Hurt as They Walk, Ride—Even Cook."

51. Quoted in Sarah N. Lynch, "Q&A: Taylor Leming, Texting Motorist," *Time*, June 26, 2008, www.time.com/time/magazine/ article/0,9171,1818190,00.html.

52. Quoted in Lynch, "Q&A: Taylor Leming, Texting Motorist."

53. Quoted in Lloyd Alter, "1/2 of yung drvrs r txtN yl drivN sEz Survey," TreeHugger.com, August 15, 2008, www.treehugger.com/files/2008/08/ half-of-young-drivers-text.php.

Chapter 4: Cameras, Video, and the Web

54. Quoted in Kevin Maney, "Baby's Arrival Inspired Birth of Cellphone Camera—and Societal Evolution," *USA Today*, January 23, 2007, www.usatoday.com/tech/columnist/ kevinmaney/2007-01-23-kahn-cellphone-camera_x.htm.

55. Maney, "Baby's Arrival Inspired Birth of Cellphone Camera—and Societal Evolution."

56. Micheal McLaughlin, personal correspondence, March 5, 2009.

57. Quoted in Julia Day, "Oil Blast Fuels Explosion in Citizen Journalism," guardian.co.uk, December 12, 2005, www.guardian.co.uk/media/2005/ dec/12/broadcasting.newmedia.

58. Quoted in Day, "Oil Blast Fuels Explosion in Citizen Journalism."

59. Chris Gaither, "John Legend's Cellphone Video Captures Giddy Celebrities Meeting the Obamas," *Los Angeles Times*, January 19, 2009, http://latimesblogs.latimes.com/ technology/2009/01/inauguration-jo.html.

60. Quoted in Alexis Akwagyiram, "Does 'Happy Slapping' Exist?" BBC News, May 12, 2005, http://news.bbc .co.uk/2/hi/uk_news/4539913.stm.

61. Quoted in Akwagyiram, "Does 'Happy Slapping' Exist?"

62. Maricelle Ruiz, "The Effects of a 'Happy Slapping' Epidemic: European Governments Crack Down on the Recording and Distribution of Violence Online," Internet Business Law Services, March 19, 2007, www .ibls.com/internet_law_news_portal_ view.aspx?s=latestnews&id=1707.

63. Quoted in ABC News on Campus, "Technology Makes Cheating 'Far More Tempting,'" ABC News on Campus, October 8, 2008. Available at http://www.groupsrv.com/ hobby/about613322.html.

64. Katz, *Magic in the Air*, pp. 94–95.

65. Quoted in Associated Press, "US Lags in Offering Cell Phone TV," Associated Press, August 18, 2008. Available at http://findtarget.com/CNN. php?/2008/TECH/ptech/08/18/ cellphone.tv.ap/index.html.

66. Tomi T. Ahonen, "Happy Birthday Mobile Content: 10 Years Old now and Worth 71 Billion Dollars," Communities Dominate Brands blog, December 5, 2008, http://communities-dominate

.blogs.com/brands/2008/12/happy-birthday.html.

67. Ryan Kim, "BART Tries Pay-by-Phone System," *San Francisco Chronicle,* January 30, 2008, www.sfgate.com/cgi-bin/article.cgi?f=/c/a/2008/01/30/BUPEUODJN.DTL&type=tech.

Chapter 5:
The Future of Phoning

68. Quoted in Craig Gold, "Cell Phone vs. Land Line," KTKA.com, March 27, 2007, www.ktka.com/news/2007/mar/27/cell_phone_vs_landline.

69. Herb Weisbaum, "Should I Ditch My Land-Based Home Phone?" MSNBC.com, March 21, 2006, www.msnbc.msn.com/id/11926475.

70. Quoted in Weisbaum, "Should I Ditch My Land Based Home Phone?"

71. Quoted in Lexton Snol, "Could Smartphones Kill In-Car GPS Systems?" *PCWorld,* November 6, 2008, www.pcworld.com/businesscenter/article/153417/could_smartphones_kill_incar_gps_systems.html.

72. Mike Elgan, "Mobile Tech Under Obama," *PCWorld,* November 7, 2008, www.pcworld.com/businesscenter/article/153506/mobile_tech_under_obama.html.

73. Brian Nadel, "Sprint's 4G Xohm WiMax: How Fast Is It?" *Computerworld,* October 10, 2008, www.computerworld.com/action/article.do?command=viewArticleBasic&articleId=9116844.

74. Brian Bergstein, "MIT Students Show Power of Open Cell Phone Systems," *Boston Globe,* May 12, 2008, www.boston.com/business/technology/articles/2008/05/12/mit_students_show_power_of_open_cell_phone_systems.

75. Tom Dunmore, "The Hunt for the Next Big Thing at CES 2009," BBC News, January 9, 2009, http://news.bbc.co.uk/2/hi/technology/7819738.stm.

76. Nokia Corporation, "Nokia and University of Cambridge Launch the Morph—A Nanotechnology Concept Device," news release, February 25, 2008, www.nokia.com/A4136001?newsid=1194251.

77. Alan Moore, "The Glittering Allure of the Mobile Society: An SMLXL White Paper," November 2008, http://smlxtralarge.com/wp-content/uploads/2008/12/the-glittering-allure-mobile-soc_final2.pdf.

GLOSSARY

amplitude modulation (AM): A type of radio broadcasting in North America on radio frequencies between 540 and 1620 kilohertz.

code division multiple access (CDMA): A digital standard for encoding cellular signals.

cell phone: A handheld device that can transmit and receive electromagnetic signals via a cellular telephone network.

cell: An area of service created by an antenna array as part of a telephone network.

coverage: The overall area of cellular telephone service that can be detected by a mobile telephone.

digital speech interpolation: A signal compression technique that recognizes periods of silence during cellular telephone calls and only transmits calls during bursts of voice activity.

frequency modulation (FM): A type of radio broadcasting in North America on radio frequencies between 88 and 108 megahertz.

global positioning system (GPS): A satellite-based system that allows users to pinpoint their location almost anywhere on Earth.

global system for mobile communications (GSM): A digital standard for encoding cellular signals.

landline: A telephone line connected to a wire-based network.

megahertz (MHz): A measure of frequency, or cycles per second, used most commonly to describe radio waves.

multimedia messaging system (MMS): The ability to encode video, audio, and/or text in a message form that embeds the content within the message, eliminating the need for attachments.

mobile phone: A handheld device that can transmit and receive via a cellular telephone network.

moblog: A blog that contains video or still images from a mobile phone.

multiplexing: A digital signal technique that allows frequencies to carry multiple cellular calls at once.

receiver: An electronic device that is capable of converting a radio signal from a transmitter into useful information.

ringtone: Any combination of notes or sounds that activates when a cellular phone receives an incoming call. Ringtones vary from simple one-note melodies to compressed versions of recorded music.

signal processor: A device that allows adjustment of an electronic signal, such as the volume of the transmission.

short message service (SMS): The ability to send and receive messages in text form using a cellular telephone.

text: An SMS message received by a cellular telephone; the process of sending an SMS message.

texter: A person who texts.

texting: The process of sending a text.

transmitter: An electronic device that sends out information on the electromagnetic spectrum, such as radio or television broadcasts, usually with the aid of an antenna.

vocoder: A device that analyzes the strength of a cellular telephone call and digitizes it into a continuously-streaming binary signal.

Books

Jon Agar, *Constant Touch: A Global History of the Mobile Phone.* Cambridge, England: Icon, 2004. The author describes smashing a cell phone to see how it works. In piecing it back together, the author discusses the history of cell phone technology.

Peter Aitken, *Camera Phone Obsession.* Scottsdale, AZ: Paraglyph, 2004. Written by a digital technology expert, this book explores some of the tips and techniques available to camera phone users, as well as ways to share photos for pleasure and business.

Aimee Baldridge and Robert Clark, *The Camera Phone Book: How to Shoot Like a Pro, Print, Store, Display, Send Images, Make a Short Film.* Washington, DC: National Geographic, 2007. The authors of this book are professional photographers who share tips on taking good photos (and how to retrieve those accidentally deleted), as well as how to connect with other camera phone enthusiasts.

Peter Glotz, Stefan Bertschi, and Chris Locke, eds., *Thumb Culture: The Meaning of Mobile Phones for Society.* New Brunswick, NJ: Transaction, 2005. A collection of essays that examine the impact of mobile phones in a variety of cultures around the world.

James E. Katz, *Magic in the Air: Mobile Communication and the Transformation of Social Life.* New Brunswick, NJ: Transaction, 2006. Fascinating stories related to the adaptations and uses of mobile phones by users of all ages.

Paul Levinson, *Cellphone: The Story of the World's Most Mobile Medium and How It Has Transformed Everything!* New York: Palgrave Macmillan, 2004. This book is a collection of stories about the impact the cell phone has had on daily life.

Barbara Pachter and Susan Magee, *The Jerk with the Cell Phone.* New York: Marlowe, 2004. This book offers an amusing yet practical examination of dealing with inconsiderate cell phone users, including everyday advice on how to deal with them and how to avoid becoming one.

Internet Sources

Tom Farley and Mark van der Hoek, "Cellular Telephone Basics," Privateline.com, January 1, 2006, www.privateline.com/mt_cellbasics.

Christine Hauser, "Picture Taken by Cellphone Leads to Sex-Crime Arrest," *New York Times,* September 18, 2008, www.nytimes.com/2008/09/19/nyregion/19arrest.html.

Inform, "The Secret Life of Cell Phones," online video, www.secret-life.org/cellphones.

Chana Joffe-Walt, "Three Generations' Views of Cell Phones," National Public Radio, December 25, 2007, www.npr.org/templates/story/story.php?storyId=17603266.

Motorola, "Making History: Developing the Portable Cellular System," Motorola, www.motorola.com/content.jsp?globalObjectId=7662-10813.

Periodicals

Tom Farley, "The Cell-Phone Revolution," *American Heritage Invention & Technology,* Winter 2007.

Beverley Head, "Yuppie Stockbrokers Found Mobile Phones Invaluable," *Australian Financial Review,* May 8, 1990.

Sarah N. Lynch, "Q&A: Taylor Leming, Texting Motorist," *Time,* June 26, 2008.

Kevin Maney, "Baby's Arrival Inspired Birth of Cellphone Camera—and Societal Evolution," *USA Today,* January 23, 2007.

Victoria Shannon, "15 Years of Text Messages, a 'Cultural Phenomenon,'" *International Herald Tribune,* December 5, 2007.

The Week, "Do Cell Phones Cause Cancer?" The *Week,* August 8, 2008.

Web Site

How Stuff Works (www.howstuffworks.com). This Web site offers explanations of how various things work, written in nontechnical language. It provides multiple pages on the technology of cell phones, including multimedia links to demonstrations of the technologies by tech experts.

INDEX

PICTURE CREDITS

About The Author

Andrew A. Kling worked as a National Park Service ranger in locations across the United States for over fifteen years. He now works as a writer and editor for a variety of nonprofit organizations and as an interpretive media developer and consultant. He enjoys hockey, technology, studying flags, and spending time with his wife and their Norwegian forest cat, Chester. Kling bought his first cell phone in 1993.